Columbia University Contributions to Anthropology

Volume IX

AN INQUIRY INTO THE QUESTION OF CULTURAL STABILITY IN POLYNESIA

By

MARGARET MEAD

AN INQUIRY INTO THE QUESTION
OF CULTURAL STABILITY
IN POLYNESIA

BY

MARGARET MEAD

AMS PRESS
NEW YORK

Reprinted with the permission of
Dr. Margaret Mead
From the edition of 1928, New York
First AMS EDITION published 1969
Manufactured in the United States of America

Library of Congress Catalogue Card Number: 70-82354

AMS PRESS, INC.
New York, N. Y. 10003

PREFACE

This study was completed in the spring of 1925, after which time the author spent nine months in the Samoan Islands. The sections dealing with Samoa have been revised in accordance with findings in the field. All statements about Samoa not definitely attributed to published sources are based upon this field work. Mr. Best's monograph upon "The Maori Canoe" and Mr. Skinner's paper upon "The Outrigger in New Zealand and Tahiti" were both published since the completion of this study. The sections dealing with canoes in New Zealand and the Society Islands have been revised in the light of this material. With these exceptions, this study is based upon sources which were published earlier than May, 1925. As the main object of this paper was the attempted solution of a general theoretical problem in the light of Polynesian material rather than the assemblage of a large number of details about various aspects of Polynesian culture, the inclusion of material from later publications, where such material would neither add nor detract from the central thesis, has not been considered necessary.

The American Museum of Natural History, New York.

May 14, 1928.

ACKNOWLEDGEMENTS

I am most deeply indebted to Professor Franz Boas under whose direction this study was undertaken and completed, and to Professor William F. Ogburn and Dr. Pliny E. Goddard to whom I owe many of the opportunities which made it possible for me to pursue my graduate study. I have to thank Mr. H. D. Skinner for his generosity in reading and criticizing this paper. For help and criticism in the preparation of the manuscript I am indebted to Dr. Ruth F. Benedict, Miss Marie Eichelberger and Miss Hannah Kahn.

TABLE OF CONTENTS

INTRODUCTION

The problem of the stability of different elements of culture, their relative sensitiveness to reinterpretation and different emphasis, is of importance in the attempted solution of two problems: the attempt to reconstruct the history of a primitive culture, and the attempt to predict the future of any given culture. The attempt to derive laws of culture, or even to formulate general tendencies, implies the need of reconstruction. Such reconstruction in the case of primitive peoples without written records is always based on incomplete data, and must be made by piecing together the evidence from skeletal remains, language, archaeological finds, and cultural forms. The relative independence of language, race and culture has been established, but there remains the problem of the relation of the different elements of culture to each other. Are ritual elements more stable than techniques? Are relationship terms more stable than moiety divisions? Are the fields of decoration more stable than the elements of the design? Or do all of these elements vary so irregularly that no one may be said to be more stable than another? Numberless questions of this character arise in any effort to piece together the history of peoples from scanty and fragmentary records.

Most of the attempts at such reconstruction have assumed one element to be more stable than another and drawn conclusions on that basis. This assumption may be either implicit in the method or expressed. Perhaps the most notable of these efforts are those of Graebner[1] and Rivers[2]; Graebner using material culture as a point of departure, derives his *kulturkreise* on the basis of a large number of observed similarities in different cultures. From the occurrence in different parts of the world of similarities of house form or club form, no matter how far apart they may be nor how unlikely any historical contact between them, he derives proof of original historical contact, so that if a sufficient number of such similarities are found between Tasmania and Tiera del Fuego, the cultures of these two remote spots are argued to have once been part of the same underlying *kulturkreis*. Such a procedure assumed tremendous stability in the form of a house or the shape of a club. Rivers, assuming that social organization, especially relationship terms, and related ritual and religious practices, are the elements of culture which are least subject to change, attempts to establish in

---

[1] Graebner, F., *Die Methode der Ethnologie*.
[2] Rivers, W. H. R., *The History of Melanesian Society*.

Melanesia a sequence of cultural types associated with different imigrant groups. Less critical attempts have been made by Elliot Smith[1] and Perry,[2] who assume a traveling complex of miscellaneous elements, (a sun cult, dual division of society, the building of megaliths, the practice of mummification, etc.) and trace the path of the people whom they believe to have possessed this civilization by the often inadequately demonstrated occurrence of any of these customs. All these attempts at reconstruction presuppose a knowledge which we do not have, a knowledge of the relative rates of change of all the elements of culture which would make it possible to reconstruct the history of civilization on the basis of any one of them, or with a group of traits of which the relative rates of change were accurately known.

Secondly, the question of relative stability, or sensitiveness to change, is important in any attempt to prophecy what the course of culture will be, what effects the intermingling of divergent cultures is likely to produce. Are immigrant peoples more likely to conserve their own social organization, while they adopt the religion of the new country? Can there be complete economic assimilation while great social dissimilarities remain? So both reconstruction of the past and prophecy of the future of culture are at a disadvantage without this necessary knowledge.

The problem might be approached from several different points of view: from that of an isolated section as compared with an exposed section of the same culture, as in the case of the Eastern and Western Eskimo groups; from that of a cultural group exposed to several different outside influences, as in the Plateau region in North America; from that of two branches of a common form developing in virtually complete isolation, as have the cultures of the Great and Little Andaman; or from the standpoint of a small migrating group, penetrating into an alien cultural setting, such as the various European immigrant groups in the United States. Any approach to the problem is further complicated by the relative complexity of the cultures under consideration, the type of divergence between them, etc. Obviously, these various aspects call for as many separate investigations. The present study will deal with relatively isolated groups, having a common cultural background, the Polynesians. Their isolation is not as complete as in the case of the Andaman Islanders, but there is a common background of culture in Polynesia to which variations may be referred as a criterion of their degree and importance.

In investigating this problem the different elements are considered as they enter into a complex of activities, rather than as separate

---

[1] Smith, G. Elliot, *The Influence of Ancient Egyptian Culture in the East and in America.*

[2] Perry, W. J., *The Children of the Sun.*

elements. It is recognized that a choice of elements which are relatively independent of one another, such as the shape of a club and the dual organization, secret societies and a certain house form, has decided theoretical advantages in the case of historical reconstructions, because their very independence of one another makes the occurrence of several of them more significant. But, while the coincidence of independent forms strengthens the argument for diffusion in the particular area, it is not as effective a technique in approaching a problem of this type as is the use of a complex of related activities. If the various religious rituals were compared with the various industrial techniques, an extremely artificial picture would be obtained as all these elements are so intimately associated in the life of the group. By selecting a complex of activities, the advantage of independence is sacrificed, and variations of the different aspects of the complex might be considered to be a function of the complex and the conclusions vitiated accordingly, — i. e. if some one element in the complex changed through accident of environment, for instance the occurrence of larger trees and the abandonment of deep sea voyages, resulting in the loss of the outrigger and so in the loss of ceremonies, taboos and decorations particularly associated with the outrigger. In reply, it may be argued that a ritual or a technique never occurs as a perfectly separate entity, but only in combination with other aspects of culture. Also, by selecting three comparable complexes, all of which have the same general ramifications in the common cultural life of an area, and analyzing the variations in these complexes in five insular cultures, an additional base for comparison is obtained. Not only may the variations be referred to the common cultural base, but they may also be referred to the completely described complex, so that the function as well as the form of each element is accurately known. For example, it is possible to describe secret societies in terms of regalia, initiation practices, and punitive activities in connection with the violation of property rights, so that they seem exactly similar, whereas if described in terms of their function in two communities, where in one case they may administer law for every member of the community, in another simply terrorize for the advantage of the members of the society, — they would be seen to have very different functions in the two communities. Thus the danger of faulty interpretation is avoided, and the elements under consideration are set off against known and comparable backgrounds.

The choice of complexes to be considered, the activities centering about canoe building, house building, and tattooing, was influenced by two considerations. In the first place, complexes were chosen which entered into the life of the people in much the same way, — all three involve a definite technique, some decorative art, functions of craftsmen and priests, ritual observances and taboos, and some relation to the important Polynesian element of rank. The choice of these particular complexes was further dictated by the type of material available for Polynesia.

The Polynesian ethnographic material is exceedingly uneven. It is difficult to compare the full and careful records of New Zealand and the recent investigations of the Bishop Museum with the testimony of travelers, missionaries and garrulous residents in other parts of Polynesia. Also, evidence of this latter type is notoriously more untrustworthy and inexact when it relates to the social organization and religion of an alien culture than in descriptions of material culture. The representation of an elaborate Marquesan tattooing design is subject to the artistic limitations of the individual who attempts to reproduce it; but the record of the attitude of a Samoan toward the cuttle fish in which he worships his god is subject to vitiation not only by lack of skill in the recorder, but also by preconceived and hostile religious attitudes. Complexes were accordingly chosen where as little of this vitiation would occur as possible. Furthermore, the choice of material culture complexes makes it possible to use the data of the earliest explorers, like Captain Cook, whose short stay and lack of acquaintance with the language made it impossible for them to describe any but the most external details of the culture.

The usual cautions concerning negative evidence are particularly in force in a field where part of the material is so heterogenous, inexpert, and sketchy. Where inferences are drawn from negative evidence, this will always be explicitly indicated, together with the grounds which seem to make such interpretation plausible in a particular instance. Such conclusions can be drawn with some margin of safety for the Maori, because the material is so abundant that it affords a possibility of checking up.

The choice of the particular island groups was also dictated by the literature available. Unfortunately, the Tongan material collected by the Bayard Dominick Expedition is not yet in print. The Paumotuas are still unexplored ground. Therefore, the choice of Hawaii, the Marquesas, New Zealand, the Society Islands, and Samoa does not claim to be the optimum methodological selection for Polynesia: it is simply the only possible choice in the light of the printed material.

The basic assumption in this study is that the elements under consideration have been common to the whole area for several hundreds of years, during which time they have been undergoing modification in each insular group. Such an assumption, however, cannot ignore the various theories concerning migration into Polynesia by different racial groups at different times. If different elements in the culture, such as curvilinear art or human sacrifices, could with any certainty be attributed to a special migration, the problem would be somewhat distorted. If the indigenous culture may be conceived as possessing all of the aspects of the complex, — that is, if some rites and some form of decoration may be assumed to have always been associated with canoe building, and the intrusive rite or style may be regarded as substituted or superimposed, then these aspects may correctly be considered the most sensitive and variable. But this is only looking at the matter from the point of view of the indigenous culture. If instead, the attention were focused upon the immigrant culture, the reverse would be true. The artistic style and religious rite which alone survived in the later culture, might be considered to be the most stable and conservative, while all the other aspects of the immigrant culture had made no impression upon the existing form. Still a third point of view is possible. If the older complex had lacked some of the elements which it now exhibits, — as a definitely priestly caste, or any device for building a house door, — these might have been accepted from the intrusive culture, and the result be a dovetailing of complementary features, no one of which need be considered more variable than another.

The complete resolution of the dilemma depends upon adequate data as to the different cultural strata in Polynesia, and this we do not have. Sullivan's[1] examination of the skeletal material had convinced him that there are three different racial strains in the present Polynesian population, in addition to extensive Melanesian influence in Western Polynesia. These different types are not evenly distributed throughout the area, nor throughout the islands of any one group. Linton[2] has attempted to correlate different features of culture with the percentage of each racial strain found in each group, but such an attempt presupposes a knowledge that we do not have, a knowledge of the stability of the elements which he discusses. Other theories, based on the study of the mythology[3] language[4], and detailed analysis of traditions[5], arrive at divergent conclusions. The most that they achieve is a possible chronology. If it is recognized that the populations of most of the islands contain these different racial strains, though in varying proportions, and that the last important migrations took place some hundreds of years ago, an investigation of the likenesses and dissimilarities of certain complexes in different parts of the area is justified. This applies to the original migrations, but does not hold for later Melanesian influence in Western Polynesia. Here, as stated above, the conclusions will differ with the point of view, but the approach of this investigation is primarily from the standpoint of the indigenous culture, from the study of three complexes, with a core which is common to the entire

[1] Sullivan, L., *The Racial Diversity of the Polynesian Peoples*, A. A. A. S., 1921.

[2] Linton, R., *The Material Culture of the Marquesas.*

[3] Dixon, R., *Oceanic Mythology.*

[4] Churchill, W., *Sisano.*

[5] Fornander, A., *The Polynesian Race;* Smith, S. P., *Hawaiki*; Williamson, R. W., *The Social and Political Systems of Central Polynesia.*

group. From this standpoint we shall adjudge those elements most stable which show the greatest similarity in the five groups, and those least stable which show the greatest dissimilarities, which serve best to individualize the different groups and so show themselves most sensitive to modifications and reinterpretations.

It is recognized that the problem cannot be solved by an investigation of one of its aspects in one area with a limited amount of material, but upon such intensive studies final solution of the question of stability will have to rest.

THE CANOE BUILDING COMPLEX

DESCRIPTION.

Canoe Building in Hawaii. — The Hawaiians had single canoes with a single outrigger[1], double canoes[2] with platforms[3] between them, and raft-like vessels built of reeds[4]. In size they varied from 24 to 70 feet long[5], from one to three feet in width, and they were about three feet in depth. The form of the Hawaiian canoe, with the exception of the reed vessels, was pointed at both ends, the main body of the keel being hewn from a single log. The sides are said by Cook[6] to have consisted of three boards about an inch thick which were lashed to the keel. He describes the extremes as raised and wedge shaped, but flattened so that the two side boards met for over a foot, forming a sort of deck. Emory[7] found sterns and bow pieces on the island of Lanai which differed from the modern canoes, in that these pieces consisted of two parts and also formed more of the hull than is usual in extant forms. The parts of the canoe were lashed together with sennit; the lashings being slightly visible on the outside and more so on the inside[8]. In the Lanai canoe each piece was rabbetted on the lower edge to fit the inside body of the canoe[7]. The outrigger has been very poorly described but seems to have been of the simplest variety. Bingham[9] describes it as having a float two-thirds the length of the canoe, with booms varying from 5 to 10 feet. One end of the float was slightly turned up like a sleigh runner, while the other end terminated bluntly like the end of a musket. The connecting booms were curved to meet the float and lashed securely to it. The distance from the stern to the rear boom was less than the distance between bow and forward boom[10], and the ends of the booms projected slightly over the other side of the canoe[11]. Meinicke[12] alone mentions the use of three connecting booms instead of two.

---

[1] Cook, II, p. 253; Bishop, p. 18; Bingham, p. 139.
[2] Bishop, p. 18.
[3] Malo, p. 173; Bishop, p. 22.
[4] Emerson, p. 18.
[5] Cook, supra; Ellis, *Journal*, p. 255; Jarves, p. 129.
[6] Op. cit.
[7] Page 90.
[8] Linton, p. 450.
[9] Bingham, p. 139.
[10] Emory, p. 90.
[11] Cobb, p. 394.
[12] Meinicke, II, p. 296.

When the canoes were rigged double, they were joined by curved rods[1] at a distance of about 6 or 8 feet[2]. These double canoes carried a platform variously described as midships[3], or in the stern[4]. Bishop[5] says the mast was stepped in this platform, but Malo[6] says that it was stepped in the starboard canoe. This platform was screened by mats[3]. Triangular sails woven from pandanus leaves were used with point downward. The paddles were oval[7] or oblong bladed[8]. Canoes were provided with a covering of mats to use in wet weather[9].

Malo[10] distinguished canoes built specially for racing and those used primarily for display. The double canoes seem to have been used for inter-island communication[11].

The work of building a canoe was prefaced by a consultation with the divining priest who consulted his god as to the choice of tree. The priest and a group of workers then went to the mountains and camped by the selected tree; here sacrifices were made to the gods. Each step in the felling of the tree and the process of shaping it into a hull was preceded by incantations from the priest. When the shaping of the log was partially complete, it was hauled down the mountain side to a specially constructed shed by the sea side, where it was finished and consecrated[12].

It is difficult to distinguish clearly between the priest whose incantations and divinations were essential to the success of the undertaking and the actual craftsmen. Remy[13] depicts the latter as a bankrupt and miserable class, and both Eveleth[14] and Malo[15] speak of the work being done by the common people. But Emerson[16] speaks of distinguished "canoemen" who would seem to have united the magic powers of the priest and the skill of the craftsman in one person. However, there is no evidence for the existence of a powerful and wealthy guild of canoe-builders, such as existed in the Samoan group.

On the other hand, the priest played an extremely important part[17]. It was he who divined by means of a dream whether the se-

[1] Malo, p. 173; Meares, p. 11.
[2] Bishop, p. 18.
[3] Emerson, p. 7.
[4] Bishop, p. 22.
[5] Page 174.
[6] Cook, II, p. 253.
[7] Ellis, *Journal*, p. 256.
[8] Cobb, p. 394.
[9] Emerson, p. 9; Malo, p. 174 and p. 179.
[10] Malo, p. 174.
[11] Bishop, p. 22.
[12] Malo, p. 168.
[13] Remy, p. 14.
[14] Page 47.
[15] Page 105.
[16] Page 19.
[17] Malo, pp. 168—172.

lected *koa* tree was sound. He had to recite the necessary incantation at each step, wreathe the fallen log with *ti* leaves, raise and again impose the specially severe taboos surrounding different stages of the work. He also made the finer measurements requisite to planning the construction of the canoe; it was he who attached the hauling lines, and he alone followed the canoe down the mountain, chanting. Finally he performed the important launching ceremony. Pupil priests[1] who desired to become full-fledged canoe-hewing priests performed an elaborate series of divination ceremonies, and if the auguries received from these ceremonies were unfavorable, their masters forbade their continuing in the calling under the threat of a supernaturally-induced death penalty.

The rites connected with canoe building fall under the heads of divination practiced by the priest and by the novice, offerings and incantations accompanying the different stages of the work which included offerings of hogs and red feathers[2], and the consecration ceremony. Human sacrifices were made occasionally in the case of the consecration of a canoe belonging to a particularly famous chief[3].

The whole procedure of canoe building was a very taboo affair. The strength of the taboo varied from periods of necessary communal labor to particular sacred steps such as striking the first blow to the prostrate trunk[4], attaching the lashings of the outrigger[5], and the consecration[6]. The place behind the canoe as it was hauled down to the sea was sacred[4]. Women, however, seem to have been present during the initial ceremonies at least[4]. The most specific prohibition imposed by the taboo was against any noise or disturbance[5]. Transgression of this rule of silence during the lashing of a royal canoe was punishable with death[5]. Suspension of all work was also occasionally ordered at the building of a particularly important canoe; — this took the usual Hawaiian form of forbidding fires to be lit, or persons to walk abroad or go fishing[7]. The infraction of the taboo of silence during the consecration ceremony meant that the canoe would be unlucky[8]. It was also strictly forbidden to enter a canoe on a taboo day[9].

The chiefs could command the services of the common people in canoe building[10], and Eveleth[11] says the king could collect canoes

---

[1] Fornander, III, p. 146.
[2] Malo, pp. 168—172.
[3] Young, p. 115.
[4] Malo, p. 169.
[5] Malo, p. 173.
[6] Malo, p. 171.
[7] Emerson, p. 6.
[8] Cheever, p. 87; Bennett, C. C., p. 13.
[9] Eveleth, p. 47; Malo, p. 105.
[10] Page 46.
[11] Young, p. 118.

2

as tribute. Human sacrifices were sometimes made at the building of chiefs' canoes[1]. A special form of lashings was reserved for the canoes of sacred chiefs[1]. The raised platform was reserved for the use of the chiefs[2]. It was punishable by death to appear on the water in a display canoe if a chief were also on the water in a canoe[1]. Eveleth[3] describes a royal procession in which the chiefs were carried in canoes on their subjects' shoulders. Malo[4] remarks that canoe racing was considered as the special prerogative of the chiefs.

The canoes of the Hawaiian were very little carved. Ellis[5] says that neither canoes nor paddles were carved at all, and Young[6] confirms this statement. But Bingham[7] mentions "pieces of thin wood, ingeniously carved" which covered a few feet as a deck and turned up some 15 inches at the end. Malo[8] explicitly refers to carved bow and stern pieces, as does the editor in the notes[9]. Greiner[10] speaks of small human figures carved in wood "which form fish spear rests on the booms of outrigger canoes." The Hawaiians were in the habit of painting their canoes black with the exception of the side strakes which were left the natural yellow color of the wood[11]. But the bulk of the decoration took the form of elaborate ornamental lashings, no details of which have survived. These lashings were of sennit and used to fasten the outrigger booms to the sides of the canoe[11] and to the float[12]. Malo[11] mentions the names of four different patterns, and Emerson[13] describes one of these as: "a highly ornamental piece of weaving, done with different colors of sennit." He also mentions the use of strips of red tapa which were flown as streamers from the royal canoes.

Canoe Building in the Marquesas. — The companion monographs by Handy[14] and Linton[15], which are the result of the investigation of the Bayard Dominick Expedition, furnish us with reliable summaries of the older literature referring to the Marquesas, and with as much additional material as it was possible to gather. The descriptions of the form and construction of the canoes are much more detailed and exact than the accounts which are available for some of the other island groups, for which a variety of authorities have been

---

[1] Malo, p. 171.
[2] Malo, p. 108.
[3] Page 69.
[4] Page 103.
[5] Ellis, *Journal*, p. 256.
[6] Young, p. 118.
[7] Page 82.
[8] Page 104.
[9] Malo, p. 178.
[10] Page 35.
[11] Malo, p. 174.
[12] Emerson, p. 15.
[13] Page 16.
[14] *The Native Culture of the Marquesas.*
[15] *The Material Culture of the Marquesas.*

cited. Therefore there will be no attempt here to cite earlier authorities; the selections of Handy and Linton will be used in all cases,
and only such of Linton's material as is comparable to information
about other groups will be duplicated here.

Linton distinguished between two types of canoe, the small
simple dugout used for fishing and the large built-up canoes. These
smaller canoes seem to have been merely the keel of the larger
boats. The natives state that their large canoes were as long as 60
feet, but there are no records of canoes of this size. War canoes and
canoes used in exploration were frequently rigged double, with a
platform, railed-in, in the case of the war canoes, made by bars
laid on the cross pieces which lashed the canoes together. The single
canoes were provided with outriggers with an indirect attachment.

The Marquesan canoe consisted of 9 parts, the underbody, bow
piece, stern piece, two side planks, and four strips used to cover the
side seams[1]. The bow piece made of a single piece of wood usually
rose at an angle of 20 to 30 degrees[2]; the side planks were of equal
thickness with the under body and from a foot to a foot and a half
in width. They were lashed to the gunwale of the canoe. Occasionally the sides of the canoe were[3] constructed of several boards
instead of only two. The lashings were visible both inside and
outside[4]. The seams were caulked with pads of cocoa-nut husk; and
feathers were used in the caulking near the ends of the canoe. These
seams were covered with strips of wood, the outside strips running
the length of the canoe, and the inside strips only covering the inner
ends of bow and stern.

The outrigger was of the indirect type. The booms were usually
two in number, occasionally three. The right ends of the booms projected beyond the sides of the canoe. The left ends were attached to
the float by means of four or six small sticks. "When four sticks were
used they were placed two on either side of the cross piece, and the
lower ends of each pair rested together; the upper ends being some
inches apart, forming what is known as the 'V' attachment." Linton
describes a canoe model in the Peabody Museum with a direct
attachment, but this may be due to the small size of the model.
Porter[5] and Quiros[6] report the use of double outriggers. Alexander[7]
reports an outrigger seen on a fishing canoe in 1898 in which each
of the two booms are thrust through square pieces of wood, and
strengthened by U shaped pieces of wood in the outside angle in the
attachment of the booms to the float[8].

---

[1] Linton.
[2] Linton and Edge-Partington: 3rd Series, No. 26.
[3] Handy, p. 157; Forster, G.: *A Voyage Around The World.* II, p. 8.
[4] Linton, p. 450.
[5] Page 102.
[6] Page 28, quoted by Linton.
[7] Page 745.
[8] This type is essentially the same as the North Java type. Vide Hornell, J.:
The Outrigger Canoe of Indonesia, p. 110.

2*

Sails were of the inverted, triangular type, of cocoa-nut leaf or possibly pandanus. The large double war canoes carried two sails, the masts being stepped in the forward end of each hull. This was the usual way of stepping the mast, by passing it up through one of the forward seats[1].

Marquesan canoes had platforms but no houses; the platform was formed of eight poles, the four lower poles being lashed to the four upper and also to the canoe. Porter[2] mentions a special central platform for the chief, and Stewart[3] speaks of a platform of small sticks. The Marquesans had war and travelling canoes, fishing canoes and ceremonial propitiatory canoes[4].

Paddles were distinguished by the presence of a knob below the blade which was connected with the blade by a short neck which curved upwards and backwards[5].

Handy has provided a detailed description of canoe building; the canoe builder, his assistants, and the priest went up into the valley where the selected tree stood. Here the priest chanted, the tree was felled, and no further work was done the first day. The second day the shaping of the canoe began; a temporary shed was erected for the accommodation of the workers. All the work on the hull was completed here; then the canoe was carried down to the sea where another house waited to receive it. Here the outrigger was made and attached. The house, the canoe itself, and the canoe builders were all decorated.

The canoe builders[6] in the Marquesas are distinguished from the priests who recited the ceremonial chants. The chief builders acted as supervisors, leaving most of the work to the friends and relatives of the owners. The owner built a house for those engaged in the construction of the canoe and provided them with food. They were paid in food, cloth, and ornaments. Skilled canoe builders often obtained great wealth and prestige. A man might become a skilled workman by inheriting his father's occupation and receiving training from him, or he might go through an apprenticeship.

The "ceremonial priest who chanted the Pu'e", or creation chant, officiated before the tree was felled[7], while it was being hauled down the mountain, and just before it was launched. The same chant seems to have been used on all of these occasions.

The rites associated[7] with canoe building, in addition to the chanting of the Pu'e, consisted in a ceremonial decoration of the canoe house, canoe, and crew, and human sacrifices in the case of a

---

[1] Linton, pp. 102—3.
[2] Porter, p. 101.
[3] Stewart, C. C.: *A Visit To The South Seas, etc.* pp. 211—212.
[4] Coan, p. 206.
[5] Linton, pp. 314—5. Similar knobs occur in Mangareva and Easter Island.
[6] Handy.
[7] Handy, pp. 154—6.

war canoe. These sacrifices were obtained by raids, made either before the canoe was launched, or soon afterwards in the canoe itself, to prove its *mana*. Sometimes a famous warrior slept in an unfinished canoe to give it *mana*[1]. Canoes were intimately associated with death in the Marquesas: coffins were often canoe-shaped, and undecorated[2]. The soul was supposed to sail away in a canoe[3], and the bodies of dead priests were placed in life-size canoes with sacrificial victims, whose function it was to row the souls to the land of the dead[4]. A ceremony was held in which a canoe, containing a small round house on a platform, a live dog, pig, and cock, breadfruit, etc., was launched upon the sea to put an end to a six-week's mourning taboo[5].

All important work in the Marquesas was taboo. Special houses were erected for the canoe builders and they were denied all association with women until they had been made "free" by bathing or incantations. The sacred work-house was burnt[6]. War and fishing canoes were taboo to all women, except priestesses and chieftainesses[7], and women were not permitted to enter the water of a lake on which a canoe floated[8].

Handy says that the skilled workmen and priests, the *tuhuna*, formed a class by themselves, and were respected and counted upon for help by the chiefs. Rank in the Marquesas, according to Handy, was largely a question of wealth, and the size of a chief's canoe might therefore be explained by his rank or by his wealth. Taboo women were not subject to the restrictions relating to fishing and war canoes. Chiefs and important priests had to have dead men to paddle their souls to Havai'i. There seems to have been no definite type of canoe reserved for chiefs. "The information given by modern natives", says Handy, "led me to believe that a large canoe was always the property of the chief of the tribe". Porter[9] relates that large canoes were often taken apart, different sections being owned and housed by different families. Handy reports that on Ua Pou the chief's war canoe was sometimes, if not always, kept on the feast place before the chief's house.

Permanent decoration of the canoes consisted of ornamental sennit lashings and of carvings. The designs for the lashings were taken from string figures. The bow and stern pieces, and often the side pieces of the large canoes were carved. The figure head consisted

---

[1] Linton, p. 302.
[2] Handy, p. 211.
[3] Fraser, p. 363.
[4] Porter, pp. 110—1.
[5] Coan, p. 206.
[6] Handy, p. 143.
[7] Op. cit., p. 156.
[8] Melville, H.; *The Marquesas Islands*, p. 147.
[9] Page 101.

of a single *tiki* face[1]. There was also a tendency to decorate the neck of the bow piece with carving in high relief, or sometimes by attaching separate figures[2], which faced in toward the canoe. The ancient form of the carving on the sides was angular geometric[3]; the more recent canoe models show a more liberal use of ovals. The designs were inscribed between zones, defined by paralled lines, which run "transversely to the long axis of the canoe." *Tiki* figures are rare and have five fingers. A canoe model showing a tiny human figure, knees flexed, is pictured by Edge Partington. The paddles were also carved, the knobs into *tiki* figures, the upper and lower surfaces into several decorated zones[4]. The longitudinal strips, covering the outside seams, were painted black, and ornamented at each lashing with tufts of white feathers. Temporary decorations consisted of cocoa-nut fronds, placed so that their ends trailed in the water, skulls[5], possibly coral and pearl shells, and cords upon which were strung tufts of human hair.

Maori Canoe Building. — In describing Maori canoes several difficulties occur. In the first place, early travelers do not distinguish clearly between the different areas in New Zealand, although later research[6] has shown that there are important differences between the material culture of different parts of the islands. In the second place, the Maori canoe underwent a decided modification soon after Cook's visit, and before the arrival of later observers. Tasman, whose principal stay was at South Island[7] reports only double canoes[8], but in 1770, Cook[9] speaks of some canoes being joined together, and of the use of outriggings. But in 1840 Polack[10], a most careful observer, could say that outriggers were unknown in New Zealand. The early double canoes were said to have been either connected by cross bars which left from two to two and a half feet between the hulls, or to have been only thirty inches apart[11], and the only information we have about the outrigger is based on a single archaeological find of a float with perforations which suggest the possibility of a stick attachment similar to that found today in Tahiti[12]. These early outrigger canoes, according to the descriptions in the mythology[13], were built of several boards lashed together, rather than the single strake characteristic of the historical type of

---

[1] The typical Polynesian conventionalization of the human figure.
[2] Model in Peabody Museum, Salem.
[3] Greiner, pp. 115—117.
[4] Linton, p. 311.
[5] Porter, p. 102.
[6] Skinner, J. P. S., Vol. XXX, pp. 77—78.
[7] Colenso, T. N. Z. I., 1894, p. 400.
[8] Tasman, p. 106.
[9] Cook, I, p. 193.
[10] Polack, I, p. 224.
[11] Best, T. N. Z. I., Vol., 48, p. 449.
[12] Skinner, H. D., Records of the Canterbury Museum, II, pt. 4, pp. 151—162.
[13] Best, T. N. Z. I., Vol. 48, p. 452.

Maori canoe. These ancient canoes carried platforms on which awnings were erected[1].

The Maoris also used a raft-like craft, constructed of bulrushes, similar to that found in the Chatham Islands[2], but this was only used as a makeshift[3]. These were sometimes 50 or 60 feet long[4]. Best[5] figures a raft-like craft from the east coast, in which the body is formed of five logs, bound together, to which an outrigger-like structure of three logs is connected by three booms, which bears a resemblance to the Samoan *amatasi*.

The typical Maori canoe of historical times was built on the dugout plan[6]. The keel was usually hewn in two or three parts later dovetailed together, and an immense strake 15 or 20 inches wide produced the desired height[7]. These side strakes were lashed to the keel with cords of flax, the lashing being visible on both sides[8], and caulked with down[7]. The seams were covered with battens which were also very long and jointed only once or twice[9]. The battens were attached by flax cords, each tie being decorated with tufts of white feathers. The stern and bow pieces were hewn out of single blocks of wood and attached separately[10]. A grating was fastened along the bottom of the canoe on which the rowers knelt, and carved braces were lashed across the canoe[11]. Savage[12] mentions partitions dividing canoes owned by two families. The sails were triangular[13], point downwards, the largest canoes carrying two[14]. They were woven of bulrush leaves[15] or of Freycinetia Banksii and flax leaves, or cordyline; provided with mast and boom; the mast was stepped in the hull. The stays were of flax[16]. The paddles were from 4 to 5 feet long[17], and usually leaf-shaped, tapering to a point — although the use of paddles for steering and as truncheons produced many variants[16]. They were often decorated with a carved *tiki* at the top and with painted or carved patterns on the blade. The blade is often thickened at the distal point[18].

---

[1] Best, T. N. Z. I., Vol. 48, p. 452.
[2] Skinner, *Material Culture of the Morioris*, passim.
[3] Best, *Maori Canoe*, p. 140.
[4] Tregear, p. 121.
[5] Best, *The Maori Canoe*, p. 71, p. 136.
[6] Best, op. cit., pp. 171—173; Cowan, p. 182.
[7] Tregear, p. 117.
[8] Best, op. cit., p. 79; Linton, p. 450.
[9] Barstow, T. N. Z. I., Vol. II, p. 74; Best, op. cit., p. 83.
[10] Hamilton, p. 11.
[11] Tregear, p. 118.
[12] Op. cit., p. 63.
[13] Op. cit., p. 120.
[14] Best, op. cit., pp. 179—184. Buller, p. 228.
[15] Best, loc. cit.; Tregear, p. 120.
[16] Hamilton, p. 14, and diagrams.
[17] Best, op. cit., p. 187; Polack, II, p. 221.
[18] Best, op. cit., p. 163.

Division of Maori canoes by function or by type of decoration produces identical classifications. The war canoes were most fully and elaborately carved; those used for traveling and fishing were plainer, with a figure-head of a human face with protruding tongue; and there was a rougher canoe, usually uncarved, but sometimes painted[1]. The largest canoes were built for war, but the other two types were not distinguished as to size.

The tree was felled by fire and partly shaped where it fell. Crops had been planted near the tree to feed the workers. Elaborate ceremonies preceded each step. The partly completed canoe was then hauled to the shore over skids and placed in a canoe-house, where the work of construction was finished. A large carved canoe was sometimes not completed for years. There was a special ceremony of launching[2].

The high development of painting and carving among the Maori produced considerable division of labor. Polack[3] says that carpenters, flax dressers, rope makers, painters, carvers, caulkers, and sail makers were employed on a large canoe, but this division can hardly be taken very seriously. The most important craft functions seem to have been those of planning the canoe and of decorating it. In connection with designing the canoe, a small model was made and submitted to the future owners (a chief or a community)[4]. Tribal specialization existed in the different types of decoration, and raids were sometimes made to obtain slaves, skilled in a particular style of carving. Parts of the work had to be done by men of rank, — notably, the refurbishing of canoes which had been used for war[5], and special parts of the shaping of the hull[4]. No record of the forms of hiring the workers or of the type of payment survives. Barstow[6] suggests that barter for canoes or for services connected with canoe building is a new development. The bulk of the heavy work was done by slaves[7].

It was the duty of the priest to see that the proper incantations were recited at each stage of the work[8]. He had to be consulted as to an auspicious day for beginning the work, — the penalty for an inauspicious beginning being bad luck for the canoe[9]. He recited at least seven incantations, — at the felling of the tree, to give power to the axes to shape the canoe, at the hauling of the canoe out of the bush, to make the heavens propitious at the beginning of a journey, to calm the sea, and on the arrival of a canoe in a strange land.

---

[1] Barstow, p. 72; Best, op. cit., p. 6; Hamilton, p. 4; Tregear, pp. 119—120.
[2] Tregear, pp. 116—119.
[3] Op. cit., p. 224.
[4] Barstow, p. 72.
[5] Earle, p. 94.
[6] P. 73.
[7] Anderson, p. 310.
[8] Hamilton, p. 9; Best, *The Maori Canoe*, III, passim.
[9] Barstow, p. 75.

There was also an incantation to give time to the paddles. The priest burnt the first chips in a sacred fire[1], and finally he performed the launching ceremony[2]. A sacred seat was reserved for the high priest in the bow of the canoe[3].

Rank among the Maori was so interwoven with the notion of religious power that it is difficult to treat the two separately. Chiefs instead of being exempted from labor were required to perform part of the work[4]. Only men who possessed supernatural power by virtue of birth might take part in felling the tree and shaping the hull[5]. When a human sacrifice was needed before felling the tree for a particularly sacred canoe, it was a chief's son who was chosen[4]. For the launching sacrifice, a slave was chosen[6]. The stern seat was reserved for distinguished persons[7]. Barstow[8] speaks of canoes being ordered and owned by individual chiefs, but there is no record of form or type of decoration peculiar to such canoes.

The varied rites associated with canoe building may be divided into: divination of an auspicious day[9], (a divination ceremony based on observations of the position of the sun and moon), rites to propitiate the forest deities[10], to ensure the successful construction, transportation, and launching of the canoe, and ceremonies to give the canoe *mana*. Best[11] records a ceremony for removing the taboo from the tree in which the chosen tree is ceremonially struck with a leaf shaped like an adze blade while a long invocation is recited. At the end of this invocation one chip was struck from the tree and this chip was carried away and burned out of hearing of the chopper's axe. The rest of the chips were kindled and a ceremonial meal cooked on the fire. According to Anderson[12] there was a ceremony for freeing the whole sacred grove from taboo before a tree could be cut. When the first chips flew from the axe, they were kindled by the priest in a sacred fire, on which a sweet potato was roasted. This potato was then placed in the gap which was left by the chips, and then removed to some hollow tree nearby, taking the sacredness of the chosen tree with it. This hollow tree now became taboo, until the completion of the canoe. A hauling ceremony described by Best[13] consisted in the preparation of two sets of food, one by a priest for the male element, eaten by the old men, and the other by a priestess

[1] Cowan, p. 180.
[2] Tregear, p. 119.
[3] Cowan, p. 49.
[4] Tregear, p. 117; Earle, p. 94.
[5] Anderson, loc. cit.
[6] Barstow, p. 76.
[7] Tregear, p. 121.
[8] Op. cit., p. 72.
[9] Barstow, p. 73.
[10] Tregear, p. 116.
[11] Best, *The Maori Canoe*, p. 44.
[12] Anderson, p. 310.
[13] Best, *The Maori Canoe*, p. 68.

for the female element, consumed by the old women. It was also customary to place fern fronds over the stump to hide the wounds of Tane[1]. Human sacrifices were offered when the tree was felled in the case of sacred canoes[2], and one or more victims were sacrificed at the launching ceremony. Barstow[3] speaks of these victims being eaten. Best[4] believes that actual human sacrifice of a ritualistic character was not the usual practice, and if it was made, the body, being that of a relative who had volunteered for the service, was not eaten. Sometimes the heart of a sacrificed sparrow hawk was substituted. According to Tregear canoes carried shrines at which offerings were made to the gods. The fate of an important canoe[5] was divined by a ceremony in which a priest consecrated a certain shrub to this purpose and then pulled it up; if the roots came up intact, the omen was propitious. The taboo was lifted from the vessel by the priest's striking the figure head with this shrub. As a completion of the rite a priestess mounted the canoe and rendered it common by contact with the female element. Sometimes the people sang a welcome chant to the canoe. All parts of the canoe were named[6]. Canoes were also associated with death among the Maori. Tregear[7] speaks of the corpse of a chief being laid on a canoe which was painted red and set up in the forest. Best[8] says a canoe was sometimes cut up after the death of its chiefly owner and part of it set up in the forest as a cenotaph. This was also done with a capsized canoe later drifting ashore as a monument to those who had been drowned. A canoe which had carried a dead body was taboo, and being useless was left on the grave. Angas[9] mentions finding in a cemetery a small model canoe, containing the property of a deceased chief. The ceremony of a propitiatory canoe has also been recorded for the Maori[10]. In this case, however, a small bulrush canoe, containing stones to represent men and cooked and uncooked food was set adrift.

The taboo surrounding canoe building was very rigid, but it differed from the Hawaiian and Marquesan type as women were allowed to approach the place where the tree was cut, the priestess participated in the ceremonies, and continence was not enjoined. Special trees were tabooed for future use, sometimes being tabooed for the use of a son[11]. Whole groves were also set apart as sacred for

---

[1] Cowan, pp. 180—181.
[2] Tregear, p. 119.
[3] Anderson, p. 315; Barstow, p. 76
[4] Best, *The Maori Canoe*, p. 112.
[5] Best, *The Maori Canoe*, p. 114.
[6] Best, p. 452; Barstow, p. 76.
[7] Tregear, p. 393.
[8] Best, *The Maori Canoe*, p. 32.
[9] Vol. 2, p. 71.
[10] Tregear, p. 219.
[11] Barstow, p. 72.

the use of canoe building[1]. The ceremonies for removing the taboo from a special tree and from the completed canoe have been described above. Food was not permitted to be eaten on the taboo quarterdeck of a traveling canoe[2]; and no food might be carried on a war vessel or a fishing canoe. The canoes of the great migration are said to have carried special canoes as tenders to convey the food.

The decoration[3] of Maori canoes falls in two classes, permanent and temporary. The permanent decorations were both carved and painted. The most elaborate vessels were richly carved, while the small fishing canoes were often merely painted. The bow and stern pieces were carved from single blocks of wood and the positions of the human figures they embodied were carefully stylized. The stern piece was from six to fifteen feet high and about fifteen inches across, and rose almost perpendicularly; the bow piece was about six to ten feet long and about two feet across[4].

At the base of the stern piece was a small carved figure, looking into the canoe, and above it at the termination of the two strengthening ribs was carved a still smaller figure. The whole stern piece was carved in a delicate filigree pattern of double spirals. The figure-head consisted of a human figure, facing forward, and a mid-rib running back from the figure, carved in the same elaborate filigree as the stern piece. Behind the transverse slab terminating the filigree there was often a small human figure facing the canoe. On the flat part of the bow piece, beneath the filigree, lay the prostrate figure of Maui. This figure-head was occasionally constructed of two pieces, — the vertical mid-board was then grooved into the block[5]. The thwarts and strakes were also carved. The second class canoes had a figure-head with protruding tongue, which was less elevated than in the case of the war canoes[6]. The forward and aft sections of the body of the canoe were elaborately decorated with painted spirals and patterns resembling those of the thigh tattooing in red, black and white[7]. The second class canoe was painted red[8], and the third class boasted neither top sides nor carved stern and bow piece. The battens which covered the seams were painted black and decorated with white feathers[6]. Rutherford[9] mentions the use of pearl shells set in the carved work, and the model in the American Museum shows these also.

The temporary ornaments consisted of feathers fastened to ropes, which streamed from the top of the stern to the surface of the

[1] Anderson, p. 310.
[2] Tregear, p. 121.
[3] Best, op. cit., p. 6; pp. 93—106.
[4] Hamilton, p. 411.
[5] Anderson, pp. 313—314.
[6] Hamilton, Plates.
[7] Hamilton, p. 15; Polack, II, p. 220.
[8] Hamilton, p. 13.
[9] *The New Zealanders*, p. 272.

water. The prow was ornamented by two long curving wands, resembling antennae, tufted with albatross feathers[1].

Canoe Building In Tahiti[2]. — The Tahitians used two types of canoes, one for short excursions which was wall-sided and flat bottomed; the other for long voyages was bow-sided and sharp-bottomed[3]. There were two types of double canoes, one used only by chiefs, the usual small outrigger canoe; and the large outrigger canoe, which carried a house, and was used for inter-island communication[4]. The double canoes[5] were formed by lashing two canoes together, and carried a platform containing a small house[6], with a roof of reeds[7]. These double canoes had high sterns and bow pieces, the latter of which were sometimes joined together in a ladder-like formation[8]. The double canoes used for war had low, covered sterns[4], and a platform projecting over the bow on which the warriors stood[9], but occasionally these had high sterns also. Cook[3] describes this platform as being raised on posts. The single outrigger canoes had a slightly curving, slender stern, and a horizontal projecting bow[10], or occasionally a high bow also[11] [12].

---

[1] Hamilton p. 13.

[2] The discussion of technological features will take in the whole group of the Society Islands, but the ritualistic features are probably only absolutely true for Tahiti, though Ellis often generalized.

Cook, Vol. I, p. 97, says, "The *Invahas* are the only boats used by the inhabitants of Otaheite; but we saw several *pahis* that came from other islands."

Ellis, Volume I, p. 181, says, "The natives of the eastern islands frequently came down to the Society Islands in large double canoes, which the Tahitians dignify with the name of *pahi*, the name for ship." (But on page 167, he uses *pahi* to mean war canoe.) "They are built with much smaller pieces of wood than those employed in the structure of the Tahitian canoes, as the low coralline islands produce but very small kinds of timber, yet they are much superior both for strength, convenience, and sustaining a tempest at sea. They are always double, and one canoe has a permanent covered residence for the crew. The two masts are also stationary, and a kind of ladder or wooden shroud," (Vide Edge-Partington, No. 30), "extends from the sides to the head of the mast. The sails are large and made with fine matting. Several of the principal chiefs possess a *pahi paumopu*, which they use as a more safe and convenient mode of conveyance than their own canoes. One canoe that brought over a chief from Rurutu, upwards of 300 miles, was very large. It was somewhat in the shape of a crescent, the stem and stern high and pointed, and the sides deep; the depth from the upper edge to the middle of the keel was not less than 12 feet."

[3] Cook, I., pp. 95—96.

[4] Ellis, *Researches*, I, p. 170.

[5] Hugenin, p. 202; Ellis I, p. 164; Bougainville, p. 266.

[6] Edge-Partington, Series I, No. 30; Cook I, p. 96.

[7] Bougainville, p. 260.

[8] Ellis, I, p. 165.

[9] Wilson, J., p. 378.

[10] Cook, I, p. 47.

[11] Edge-Partington, Series I, No. 29.

[12] Christian, pp. 199—200, discusses three types: "The *va'a* or ordinary canoe of small size." "The *a'ria* or double canoe." "The *pahi*, or raft boat, which somewhat resembles the balsa of ancient Peru, and the cata-

Three variations occurred in the construction of the keel. The war canoes were flat sided, the sides consisting of but one broad plank lashed to the keel[1]. The hull of the double canoe on the other hand resembled in cross sections the print of a spade[2], on a playing-card. The island-canoes had extra wash-boards on each side[3]. The canoes varied from 10 to 72 feet in length, but the greatest width was about three feet[2], and they were from three to four feet deep[3]. The platforms were sometimes ten or twelve feet long, and even wider, the house five or six by six or seven feet. The stern sometimes rose as high as twenty-four feet[4]. The hull of most of the canoes was built up of a number of planks sewed together with sinnet, and caulked with cocoa-husks and bread-fruit gum[5]. There is some doubt as to whether this sewing was visible or invisible[6]. The keel itself was often made in several pieces[4]; the bow was formed of a solid piece which formed the front of the hull also. The sterns were slender, curving posts, sometimes joined together[4][5].

The characteristic form of the Tahitian outrigger is a weaker development of the stern boom. The bow boom extends further, over the right side of the canoe[7], and is a curved piece, which Ellis[8] describes as elastic, and Hugenin[9] as forming an arc. The attachment of the bow boom is the double V attachment; the sticks are sunk into perforations in the float, bent in until they lie flat against the float, and lashed in place with sennit; "the cord passing through the perforations in the float and back to a point on the boom inboard from the stick[10]." The stern boom might be directly inserted, tied[11], or tied to a very small peg[12], inserted in the float[10]. Cook gives the length of the boom as six to ten feet[13]; Bougainville[14] as four to five feet.

---

marans of the Chatham Islands, also called *pahi* by the natives, the construction of which allows the water to wash through the body of the vessel. . . . The Tahitian *pahi* was often quite 80 feet in length, broad in the middle, very carefully and neatly planked over inside, forming a sort of rude bulkhead or inner casing and had a lofty carved stern rising up into one or two substantial posts." (This last description suggests European influence, but he states specifically on page 199 that "When Europeans came to Tahiti there were three sorts of vessels in use.")

[1] Wilson, p. 378.
[2] Cook, I, pp. 95—97; Wilson, p. 377.
[3] Ellis I, p. 169.
[4] Wilson, p. 377.
[5] Ellis I, p. 165; Tyerman and Bennett, p. 256.
[6] Linton, p. 450; Best, *The Maori Canoe*, p. 86.
[7] Ellis I, p. 171; A. M. N. H. model 80. 0/3045 a, and 80.0/3054; Hugenin, p. 200; Bougainville, p. 259.
[8] Ellis, I, p. 171.
[9] Hugenin, p. 200.
[10] Skinner, H. D., "*The Outrigger in New Zealand and Tahiti*." J. P. S, Vol. 36, p. 363.
[11] A. M. N. H. Model 80.0/3045 a.
[12] A. M. N. H. Model 80.0/3054.
[13] Cook, p. 196.
[14] Page 259.

A peculiar feature of the Tahitian canoe is the development of the projection of the major outrigger boom beyond the opposite side of the canoe[1]. Ellis[2] describes this board as projecting five or six feet, and elevated four or five feet above the water, having a railing along the side. Upon this a native stood in rough weather, to balance the canoe[1],[3]. Wilson[4] describes this as being a stage two feet wide and ten or twelve feet long; and Forster's drawing[5] shows this board as additional to the outrigger boom. All the descriptions mention tying the shrouds to this projection. It undoubtedly is a variant of the "weather platform" found in Samoa. Canoes over 25 feet long carried sail[6]; the mast was less than the length of the canoe. Double canoes carried two masts[7]; the sails were of the inverted triangle shape, but differed from those of Eastern Polynesia in having the upper end of the boom recurved[8]. They were woven of pandanus leaves[7] and surrounded by a frame of wood[6]. The sails of the island-canoe resembled half an oval, with the straight side placed next to the mast[9]. The mast was stepped in a batten placed across the canoe[7], nearly amidship in single canoes, and about one-third from the end in double canoes[10]. Hugenin[11] pictures and Wilson[10] describes an extra sprit "laced up and down the after leech, and reaching one-third higher than the mast head." The paddles were plain and oblong bladed[12] with a knob at the end of the blade[13].

Functionally Ellis[12] distinguishes between traveling and fishing canoes, war canoes, the special double canoes used by the chiefs, and the sacred canoes of the priests.

The trees for canoe building were cut down and partly shaped in the mountains; then brought down to the shores and finished in a special shed[14]. All the parts were fitted together first, and then taken apart, and rubbed with sand and coral. Wilson[15] gives a detailed account of the building of the war and sacred canoes. These were built by a general levy passed down from chiefs through their landholders to the tenants, who provided the material to pay the workmen and the labor for the heavier parts of the work. Feasts were made at several stages of the work.

---

[1] Page 259.
[2] Ellis, I, p. 171.
[3] I. p. 171.
[4] Page 379.
[5] Forster, J., p. 460.
[6] Cook, I, p. 96.
[7] Ellis, I, p. 174.
[8] Linton, p. 317.
[9] Ellis, I, p. 174; Cook, I, p. 47.
[10] Wilson, J., p. 379.
[11] Page 201.
[12] Ellis, I, p. 171; Cook, I, pp. 95—97.
[13] Forster, G., Vol. II, p. 8.
[14] Ellis, I, p. 175.
[15] Pages 377—8.

There was a special group of carpenters[1] and some division of labor[2], especially in the ornamentation and sail making. Some of the canoe builders were attached to the services of the principal chiefs, while others were especially hired, paid with hogs and cloth, and fed and housed by the owner, during the construction of the canoe. The account of the feasts given at each stage of the work suggest the Samoan type of payment, but Wilson rather emphasises the religious aspect.

The priest seems to have officiated at each of these ceremonies[3], and the consecration took place at the altar of the chief in whose district the canoe was built. At the consecration of one of the sacred canoes, (these contained houses and shrines with images of the gods decorated with red feathers)[4] the king officiated also.

The accompanying rites consisted of prayers to the gods of the craft[5] and of the chief[6], and to "Eatoo"; these were offered before the tree was cut down, at the commencement of the construction, and when each layer was made fast[7]. When the canoe was finished, hogs were strangled and offered at the altar, accompanied by young plantain trees. The entrails were eaten and the rest of the flesh left to putrefy. At the consecration of the sacred canoes, they were decorated with cloth, breastplates and red feathers, and hauled to the *marai*[8]. On this occasion a human victim was offered. The eye of the victim was offered in pantomime to the king, and the body interred in the *marai*. Hogs were also offered, and the decorations of the canoe were presented to the king. Canoes so consecrated were afterwards sacred to the services of the god[3]. The canoes of the Areois society contained special altars[9]. Canoes were named after some particular event in which they had played a part[10].

The chief conducted the building of large canoes on the basis of a feudal levy[11], which passed down through the landed farmers to the tenants. Chiefs used a special type of double canoe[12]. When a canoe was built, sacrifices were offered to the gods of the chief. The chief occupied the house built on the platform of the canoe, which could be taken apart and taken ashore for the chief's use[13]. The "king", or sacred chief, took part in the consecration of the

---

[1] Wilson, pp. 377—8.
[2] Ellis, I., pp. 175.
[3] Ellis, I, p. 176.
[4] Tyerman and Bennett, I, p. 244; Ellis, I, p. 169.
[5] Moerenhout, Vol. I, p. 252.
[6] Ellis, p. 176.
[7] Wilson, pp. 378—79.
[8] Sacred place, sometimes stone enclosure containing altar.
[9] Ellis, I, p. 316.
[10] Ellis, I, p. 163.
[11] Wilson, J., p. 378.
[12] Ellis, I, p. 169.
[13] Cook, I, p. 196; Wilson, pp. 377—79.

sacred canoes. Ellis[1] says the rank and dignity of a chief were indicated by the size of the canoe, the decorations, and the number of rowers.

There is no mention of a taboo connected with building a canoe[2]. When men and women traveled, their food was carried in separate canoes[3].

The permanent decorations of the canoe consisted of carvings on the stern and bow pieces. The body of the canoe was not ornamented[4]. The stern pieces were very slender and carved in the round, with one small figure above another[5]. Those of war canoes had a human head or other grotesque figure on the figure-head and a bird's head on the stern. These carvings were more realistic than those of the Maori or the Marquesan and there was much less attention given to incidental ornamental detail.

Canoe Building In Samoa[6]. — The Samoan canoe had been so modified by borrowing from Fiji, by way of Tonga, that scarcely any of the original canoes were extant at the time of discovery[7]. The modification introduced from Fiji was the permanent attachment of two canoes, one smaller than the other[8], upon which a permanent platform extended in such a way as to give the appearance of a raft, supported by two keels. Samoa shared with Fiji, Tonga and the smaller islands in the Society Group the manufacture of canoes out of many pieces, joined by sennit sewing. The discrepancy between the size of the two canoes is believed by Best[9] to have been characteristic of the original Samoan double canoe. The Samoans had also large single canoes with single outriggers[10], a small outrigger canoe, and Krämer and Demandt treat the bonito boat separately[10], although it is really only a small outrigger canoe[11]. The Samoan single canoe had a sharp cut-water[11], but this does not seem to have been the case with the two canoes in the case of the double canoe: these show a slow upward curve to a broad blunt bow and stern. The larger canoes were not built up from a dug-out log by the addition of side-pieces, but were sewn together by a method of sennit lashes which rendered the seams invisible from the outside. This was accomplished by leaving the edges of the constituent board

---

[1] I, p. 176.
[2] Tyerman and Bennett, II, p. 53, mention a man and a woman working on a canoe but this was in 1821, and may not be significant.
[3] Wilson, J., p. 35.
[4] Ellis, I, p. 175.
[5] Ellis, I, p. 168; Wilkes, I, p. 279; Forster, J., p. 459; Edge-Partington, Series I. No. 30.
[6] Statements to which no footnotes are appended are based upon the author's own field work in Samoa.
[7] Thompson, B., p. 294; Brown, G., p. 340.
[8] Krämer, II, p. 251; A. M. N. H. Model 80.0/115 a.
[9] Op. cit., p. 449.
[10] Demandt, p. 72; A. M. N. H. Model 80.0/3016 a; Krämer, II, p. 243.
[11] Krämer, II, p. 253; Hood, p. 406; Demandt, p. 73.

thicker than the rest of the board. (These boards were of irregular size and shape.) The stitches passed through the protuberant rims[1], left at the edge of the boards. The edges of the boards were fitted carefully together[2], the seams being caulked with bread-fruit gum[3].

The outrigger was usually of the type known as the indirect V attachment. There were sometimes two, and sometimes three booms, and these were strengthened by cross pieces or diagonal poles. In addition to the short sticks forming the double V, cords connected the float with these cross bars[4]. Demandt's[5] figures of the bonito boat show two booms, and an abortive one which does not quite touch the float. The float was pointed only at the forward end, and was triangular in cross section[6]. It was attached so that the distance from the rear end of the float to the stern end of the canoe was less than that from the forward end of the float to the bow of the canoe. Krämer[7] gives diagrams of a direct inserted attachment, formed by the use of a curved boom. It is notable that while the Samoans borrowed Fijian raft-like boats, they did not borrow the Fijian technique for overcoming the one-way limitations of the single outrigger by changing the position of the mast[8]. Instead they developed a "weather platform[9]," a narrow rim, or extending board on which the native stood to balance the canoe in rough weather. This may be a very crude form of the heavily buttressed projecting side of the Marshall Island canoe[10]. The platform[4] on the Samoan canoe was raised on heavy transverse blocks of wood; the floor consisted of wide planks lashed together, and square openings were left over each canoe. The mast was stepped in the larger canoe. The distance which the platform was elevated above the canoe equalled the depth of the canoe. On this a house, triangular when viewed from the bow, was erected, with a thatched roof slanting to the floor on one side. Although the form of the double canoe is believed to be of Fijian origin, this slant-roofed house is credited to the Manu'a Archipelago in nomenclature and native theory. The vertical side of the house was against the mast. Four posts at the corners of this structure were surmounted by another small platform. The whole effect was of a much taller vessel[11] than those of Eastern Polynesia. The sail was not triangular with the apex at the base as in the eastern islands, but was supported by a yard which

[1] Krämer, II, p. 253; Hood, p. 406; Demandt, p. 73.
[2] Brown, G., p. 349.
[3] Turner, p. 163.
[4] A. M. N. H. Model 80.0/3015, 80.0/115 a; Krämer, II, p. 251; Turner, p. 164.
[5] Page 73.
[6] A. M. N. H. Model 80.0/116; Demandt, loc. cit.
[7] *Hawaii, Ostmikronesien und Samoa*, p. 415.
[8] Thompson, B., p. 294.
[9] Fox, J. R. A. I., Vol. 4, p. 430; Wilkes, I, p. 199; Krämer, II, p. 251.
[10] A. M. N. H. Model 80.0/346.
[11] A. M. N. H., Model 80.0/3015, 80.0/115 a; Krämer, p. 251.

hung from the mast head[1][2]. It was of coarsely woven matting, surrounded by a rim of wood. Distinctions in function were based on the use of the canoe for fishing, traveling, and by chiefs[3]. Also there was a play-boat, called an *amatasi*[4], a light craft with a heavy outrigger float, which carried a sail. The distance between the float and the canoe was covered by a lattice work platform with two crossed logs as a base. This type of canoe had a heavy cut-water, and the float extended from about one-quarter of the way from the bow to the stern. The paddles were leaf-shaped, — the bulge occurring about one-third of the way from the top of the blade[5].

The procedure of Samoan canoe building was exceedingly elaborate, hinging entirely upon the relations between future owner and professional builders[6]. The builders were first formally engaged by the present of a valuable mat. After extensive borrowing among his relatives and planting crops to support the builders, the owner summoned the workmen. The workmen brought with them the logs which had been cut and left to season at the time of the initial engagement. A special shed was erected in which the canoe was built. Payments were made at stated intervals during construction. The launching was followed by a display trip from village to village.

The canoe builders in Samoa were a definite guild[7][8]. Recognition as a master workman depended upon the satisfactory erection of a house or building of a canoe, of sufficient importance to have all the ceremonious payments made with due formality. The owner of the canoe was forced to treat the builders with great consideration; the head of the family was expected to sit with them and prepare sennit for their use. The builders brought their wives and children with them, and these were fed at the expense of the owner. If the heavy payments, which the workmen received at stated intervals were not satisfactory to them, they left in anger and no other carpenter might take up the work, under the penalty of being robbed of his tools and severely beaten by his confrères[9]. The whole village would assist the carpenters in enforcing this discipline. The final payment, called *umu sa*, or sacred oven, was the occasion of a festival when the finest mats were presented one by one, with elaborate recitation of their pedigrees. This was a very important socio-ceremonial occasion, not a religious one. The relatives of the owner polished the canoe with coral, after the departure of the workers. Priests had no

---

[1] A. M. N. H., Model, 80.0/3015, 80.0/115 a; Krämer, p. 251.
[2] Linton, p. 317.
[3] Stair, p. 57.
[4] Krämer, II, pp. 268—269. For comparison, see Best, *The Maori Canoe*, p. 136.
[5] A. M. N. H. Model 80.0/3016 a.
[6] Stair, pp. 147—152; Turner, p. 62; Brown, G., p. 250.
[7] Stair, p. 147; Turner, p. 62; Brown, G., p. 250.
[8] This was also the case among the house builders.
[9] Brown, G., p. 250.

function in connection with canoes. The place of work was formally taboo to intruders[1] who had no business at the place of work. This did not extend to women coming on errands to the workers. No other taboos are recorded in connection with canoe building. Continence was enjoined upon the builder of a fishing canoe the night before the canoe made its maiden voyage. Women were at all times forbidden to touch a bonito canoe. A canoe which was named for a family god could not be sold[2]. Canoes occasionally carried the symbols of a village god[3]. The bodies of chiefs were placed in canoes which served as coffins[4]. No mention is made of human sacrifices or other religious rites, except in one myth which records how a legendary chief of an unknown island launched his canoe over human bodies.

The decked part of the canoe was the seat of honor for men of rank[5], and a chief's canoe carried conchshells which were blown when he passed a village[6].

The Samoan canoe was very little carved[7]. What carving there was seems to have been a series of geometrical grooves, or triangles[8], on the sides of the canoe. Occasionally rude figure-heads occurred, which were carved in the image of a dog, bird, or human figure, the traditional coat-of-arms of a particular village[9]. The distinctive decorations were rows of white shells running along a series of projections on the bow deck and stern deck and along the outrigger[10]. Krämer[11] pictures a stern piece decorated with angular geometric incisions arranged in zones. Temporary poles supporting images of birds or dogs were sometimes erected in a canoe[12].

ANALYSIS OF CANOE BUILDING.

The typical Polynesian canoes are the single outrigger canoe and the double canoe with more or less temporary connecting platforms. Canoe building is a specialized occupation throughout the area and the canoe itself enters into the social stratification and the religious patterns in varying degrees. Some form of decoration is found on the canoes of all the groups. The smallest form of the single outrigger canoe, the simple dug-out, was almost identical throughout the area, although the type of decoration, if it was

---

[1] Stair, p. 149.
[2] Turner, p. 18.
[3] Brown, G., p. 250; Erskine, p. 60.
[4] Pritchard, p. 159.
[5] Turner, p. 163; Hood, p. 101.
[6] Turner, p. 165.
[7] Greiner, p. 61.
[8] A. M. N. H. Models, in preceding notes.
[9] Turner, p. 164.
[10] Hood, p. 46; Wilkes, I, p. 199; Turner, p. 165.
[11] Vol. II, p. 261.
[12] Turner, p. 191.

decorated, followed the group pattern, — and the Samoan dug-out had the characteristic sharp cut-water. Sails made of coarse woven mats were used in all the groups; these sails could not be reefed, being of the inverted triangle type, except in Samoa. Technologically the canoes were all constructed by lashing additional wooden parts to a basic dug-out keel, by means of cords (made of sennit except in New Zealand). In Samoa this lashing was invisible from the outside. The number of side pieces varied from the immense single strakes of the Maori canoe to the small irregular patches used in some of the smaller islands of the Society group. This divergence seems to have been partly a question of the size of the available trees, although single strakes and small patches are both found in the Societies. The keels of the longer canoes were occasionally made of one to three pieces of logs joined together. There are only a few significant variations. The Samoan canoe, under Fijian influence, had adopted the permanent raft-like platform; the Maori canoe, due perhaps to increased size and resulting stability, discarded the outrigger, and the canoes of Samoa and Tahiti added the "weather-platform." The outrigger attachment varies from the double V form of Samoa[1] and the Marquesas, through the intermediate Society Island type, with its double V forward attachment and simpler stern attachment. What evidence we have suggests that the Maori outrigger was of this form also. The Marquesan and Maori canoes had battens to cover the seams. The most important difference in technique is between the five piece canoe, the major portion of which is hewn from a single log, and the plank canoe, built up of many pieces of board. The Society Islands and Samoa used the second type at the time of discovery, while the Hawaiians, Maori and Marquesans used the canoe of the five piece type[2]. One of the two canoes forming the Samoan double canoe was larger than the other and the mast was stepped in the larger canoe. Houses were built on Samoan and Tahitian canoes, and are reported for the propitiatory canoes of the Marquesans and on Maori canoes traditionally; canopies formed by awning stretched over supporting posts are recorded for the Hawaiian and Tahitian canoes. The bulrush raft-canoe seems to have been outside this general complex. It is reported definitely from New Zealand and Hawaii and possibly occurred in Tahiti. It is noteworthy that a small vessel of this type was used by the Maori as a propitiatory drift offering, and that the analogous Marquesan drift offering was a canoe carrying a round house, although the typical Marquesan canoe did not carry a house.

The distinction between canoes used for different purposes seems to have been a purely usual one between canoes used for travelling. fishing and war. Chief's canoes were larger in all the groups, especial-

---

[1] The simple inserted form also occurred in Samoa.

[2] The use of more than five pieces is mentioned for all three of these groups, however, so this difference would seem to be a later development.

ly decorated in Samoa and Tahiti, with exclusive right to certain sennit decorations in Hawaii. Canoes differently constructed and reserved for sport are reported for Hawaiia and Samoa only[1]. Canoes dedicated to a god and sacred to the use of the priests of that god occur in Tahiti and are recorded also among the Moriori.[2]

The differences in the importance and prestige of the craftsmen in the different groups was enormous. In Hawaii the planning and all of the most skilled work was done by the ceremonial priests; skill was a question of special religious vocation, and the priest whose auguries were unfavorable was forbidden to engage in canoe building, without respect for his proficiency. Canoe builders were a starveling class, poorly paid, and little esteemed. In the Marquesas the skilled workers were separated entirely from the priests, whose functions were of a strictly religious character. The workers were housed and fed during the construction of the canoe, and handsomely recompensed. The marks of their participation in a sacred occupation still clung to them, however, for they were tabooed throughout the course of the work, living removed from all connection with women, in a separate house built for this special purpose. Skilled artisans were classed with the priests as belonging to a loose, slightly organized class in society, *tuhuna*. Among the Maori the picture is blurred by the coincidence of rank and religious power in the same individual. Furthermore, the high development of carving and painting called for greater specialization and set more of a premium upon talent as distinguished from training. Cases are recorded of raids conducted primarily to obtain slaves skilled in the execution of the particular type of decoration for which a special tribe had become famous. The elaborately carved bow and stern pieces were sometimes the work of years and seem to have been left in the hands of special artists. The designing of a large canoe was also a matter for the expert who was sometimes summoned from a great distance; but the actual construction of the canoe was not left in the hands of the experts. Besides the definite ritual acts which were performed by ceremonial priests, there were many parts of the work which must be done by men of rank who possessed *mana*. So we get here this curious reverse of the Hawaiian picture, where all work was sedulously avoided by individuals with any pretention to rank. The parts of the construction of a Maori canoe demanding communal labor were performed by slaves. Skill here seems to have been an individual matter — not institutionalized to any great extent. In Tahiti canoes built for districts or chiefs were built by a sort of feudal levy in whi h the materials were provided and the heavy work, such as felling the trees was done by different tenant groups. We know less about the Tahitian canoe builders, but we know they were a definite class,

---

[1] The Hawaiian play-canoe was long and slender, built primarily for display. In Samoa the *amatasi* was an intrusive Fijian form.

[2] Skinner, H. D., *The Material Culture of the Moriois*, I, p. 116.

members of which attached themselves to the service of important
chiefs, while others were hired by regular payments of hogs and
cloth. These payments were made at different periods in the con-
structions of the canoes, at which times offerings were made to the
gods of the profession and of the chief. The sequence of payments
is reminiscent of the Samoan pattern, but the occurrence of a definitely religious rite at each stage is more like Hawaii. The Samoan
canoe builders were far more powerful and important than those of
any of the other groups. Building a canoe was largely a question
of accumulating enough property to engage sufficient workers,
who brought with them a train of apprentices and dependents, and
took the actual construction entirely into their own hands. The
ceremonial elaboration here is concerned not with mollifying offen-
ded deities or entreating the favor of divine patrons of the profession,
or the chiefs, but with conciliating the arrogant and powerful guild
of canoe builders. Set speeches and kava ceremonies which amounted almost to a social ritual were prescribed for each step in the
negotiations. An important member of the household, either the
chief himself or a delegated representative, was expected to sit with
the builders, administer to their needs, and ensure their affability.
If the builders were dissatisfied at any stage, either with the treatment or the payments they received, they would discontinue the
work; so conscious was their sense of professional solidarity, that
no other workers would dare to take up the construction. The high
rate at which their services were reckoned was uncomplicated by
any parallel function, of priest or chief, and they enjoyed undisputed
and tremendous prestige.

The importance of the priest varies almost inversely to the importance of the craftsmen, but this correlation is not perfect. In Hawaii
the priest had charge of the divination in which, by means of a special
ritually-sought dream, the gods advised him as to the soundness of
the selected tree. He performed the series of ritual acts and the
accompanying incantations, at the felling, shaping, hauling and
launching of the canoe, and also did all the planning and the
particularly skilled work connected with the construction. Men
entered an apprenticeship, not to the master craftsman as in Samoa,
but to the canoe-building priest, of much *mana*, and their vocation
was tested on religious, not practical grounds. In the Marquesas the
priestly function consisted of the recitation of the *Pu'e*, the chant
which united the new-made canoe with all things that had been
made before. The priest accompanied the workmen, chanting at the
felling of the tree, while it was hauled down the mountain-side and
at the launching ceremony. The emphasis seems rather to have
been upon the priest as the exponent of the religious aspect of all
work than upon his intimate connection with canoe building as
such. Among the Maori many of the most sacred functions were the
prerogatives of those of high birth, instead of belonging to those who

had made a vocation of priest-craft. Thus, just as the skilled crafts-man had to yield to the supernatural fitness of the high-born man of *mana*, so the most sacred parts of the construction itself were done by chiefs, not by priests. But a multiplicity of activities still remained to the priest. He took the auguries for an auspicious day to begin the work — not by a dream as in Hawaii, but by calculations based on the position of the moon — he removed the taboo from the chosen tree, and recited the incantations appropriate to each stage of the work. The phraseology of these incantations suggests the Hawaiian, but the position of the priest is not as much emphasised, because so much of the work was performed by men of rank. The priesthood in Tahiti was a more institutionalized matter. The priest was called in to make offerings at each stage of the work, and officiated at the community altar when canoes specially dedicated for war or for the service of the gods were consecrated. At the dedication of the sacred canoes a religious function was taken over by the most sacred chief, or "king", who was offered the eye of the human victim sacrificed on these occasions. The whole emphasis is on a priest who serves a definite altar, and makes offerings there to sanctify a special canoe. Furthermore, the priests had their own canoes, in which they erected shrines, and these specially decorated craft were an important element in the Tahitian fleet. In Samoa no religious rites have been recorded. The place of work was taboo, that is, reserved from unseemly interruption. But the uninstitutionalized shamanistic priest had no function.

The religious rites show certain similarities. The procedure as such, the division into stages marked by religious observances, seems to be in part mechanically determined by the type of construction. In those groups where the tree was felled and partly shaped in the mountains, the rites centered about a five-fold pattern of felling, steps in shaping, hauling to the shore, finishing steps, and launching. In Tahiti and Samoa, where the canoes were constructed of smaller units of wood the stages chosen for special observance, — in Samoa only by ceremonial payment of the workers, in Tahiti by offerings to the gods and payment of the workers, — were the various steps in the actual construction of the canoe. In these latter groups, the selection of the tree and the process of conveying the tree down to the shore have lost their significance, both actually and in ceremonial practice.

If the accompanying rites are studied in detail, great variation is found. In Hawaii the divination of the suitability of the tree is made by the priest sleeping in front of his shrine, where he is supernaturally advised in a carefully defined dream. Among the Maori, divination is based on the movements of the moon, and the roots of a plant. In Hawaii, New Zealand and the Marquesas the group of workers repair to the mountains and offerings are made. But in the Marquesas the erection of the taboo house for the workers assumes a ceremonial significance, which is absent elsewhere, while in Hawaii the hewing of the canoe and the necessary charms are done together by the officiating priest. Among the Maori the emphasis is on removing the sacredness from the selected tree, the hewn log, and the finished canoe. The binding of the outrigger to the canoe is the specially taboo operation in Hawaii; and the place behind the canoe was sacred to the priest who followed it down the mountain, chanting as he went. Among the Maori the whole group engaged in the operation sing canoe-hauling songs to liven their work, although a canoe hauling incantation was also recited.

Human sacrifice occurs in all of the groups except Samoa, but with varying coincidence. In Hawaii a sacrifice was made at the launching of the war canoe of some great chief. The basis on which the victim was selected is not recorded[1]. In the Marquesas the completed war canoe was dispatched on a raid to secure sacrificial victims to give the canoe *mana*, or occasionally raiding parties were sent out to obtain sacrifices for the launching of a large canoe. Here the victims seem to have been chosen from enemy tribes. Among the Maori, at the building of a great chief's canoe, a human victim was buried beneath the tree. This sacrifice required a victim of rank; sometimes one of the chief's own children was selected. At the launching of the canoe, on the other hand, slaves were sacrificed and eaten; the object seems to have been an enhancement of the festivity of the occasion more than of the *mana* of the canoe. In Tahiti human sacrifices were made only when a sacred canoe was dedicated to Eotea; at other times offerings of hogs were substituted. The eye of the victim, in conformance to the Tahitian mock-cannibalistic pattern, was offered to the "king."

The taboos connected with canoe building show as wide a variation — the taboo pattern in each group being quite distinct and unmistakable. Unfortunately we have no record of taboos from Tahiti except the prohibition against the profane use of canoes dedicated to Eotea. A similar prohibition existed in Samoa, where canoes named after the gods could never be sold[2]. In Hawaii the taboos surrounding canoe building were most rigorous. They were characterized by periods of great sacredness followed by intervals of relative laxity. The most serious transgression of the taboo was in the form of noise or disturbance, punishable in the case of the lashing of a "royal" canoe with death. The place behind the canoe, as it was hauled down the mountain, was taboo, and only the priest might walk there. The mythology tells of long taboos

---

[1] Malo, pp. 211—212, mentions that the human sacrifice for the Luakine ceremony in the ritual of Ku must be a malefactor. The choice of a sacrifice of this type for one of the most important ceremonies may be significant in this connection.

[2] This taboo has particular point in Samoa, because canoes were regular objects of barter.

imposed during the building of specially sacred vessels — these follow the typically Hawaiian pattern, in which all persons are forbidden to walk abroad, to enter a canoe, to light a fire, or engage in any work. In the Marquesas, where all work was taboo, the chief prohibition was against all contact with women. All of those engaged in the operation were purified by bathing or charms before they began their labor; they lived in a sacred house; their food was taboo and they were denied all intercourse with women. Women were not allowed to enter a canoe or even to bathe in a lake in which a canoe floated. If a fishing canoe were profaned by the touch of a woman, human hair must be burnt on the bow to purify it. Among the Maori there is a still different pattern. Here the grove of trees, sacred to the uses of canoe building, is taboo; and this taboo must be removed from the selected tree and transferred to another tree[1]. In addition to this, parts of the work were taboo except to those possessing the supernatural powers inherent in priesthood or in rank. Food was taboo upon fishing vessels and on the quarter-deck of war-vessels. (In Tahiti the food of men and of women had to be carried in separate canoes on a journey.) In Samoa the operation was taboo against intrusion of any sort, and men of all ranks had to pass by another way. Thus while various taboos may be said to attach themselves to canoes and canoe building all over the area, their prohibitions are so varied and so thoroughly integrated with the taboo patterns of the various groups that very little similarity is discernable.

The connection between canoes and rank is partly inevitable and partly incidental. All over the area the chiefs had the largest and most highly decorated canoes, the most desirable seat on the front deck or the platform, beneath the awning or in the house was reserved for the chiefs and their families. This would seem to be the logical consequence of the wealth and prestige of chiefs in Polynesia. In Hawaii a common man was forbidden to put off from shore in a display canoe if a chief were out on the water; canoe racing was considered to be the prerogative of the chiefs; a special lashing was reserved for the "royal" canoes, and intrusion on their construction was punished with death. In the Marquesas the chiefs usually owned the canoe, and these war canoes were kept in a canoe-house in the chief's establishment. But this seems to have been more a trusteeship for the group, rather than strictly a chiefly prerogative.

The permanent decoration of canoes had developed into a definite style in each group. The Hawaiian canoes were very little carved and their characteristic decorations were elaborate sennit lashings in different colors. The keel of the canoe was painted black, and the upper strake left the natural yellow color of the wood. In the

---

[1] See page 25.

Marquesas an elaborate and highly individualized style of carving was found. The stern and bow pieces of large canoes were always ornamented and sometimes the side pieces. The figure-head consisted of a single flat *tiki* face, and the neck of the bow piece was sometimes ornamented with small figures carved in high relief, or attached. These are the essentials of the Maori figure-head, although worked out so much more elaborately in New Zealand. The sides and stern of the canoes were carved with angular geometric and also with curvilinear designs arranged in zones between parallel lines running transversely to the axis of the canoe. Ornamental colored sennit lashings were also used. Among the Maori the typical stylization of the human figure was supplemented by a wealth of incidental ornamental detail built around the double scroll. The bow-piece was a highly conventionalized arrangement, and the stern piece consisted of the characteristic scroll filigree work. The sides of the canoes were also painted in curvilinear patterns, resembling those used in thigh tattooing. The smaller canoes, which were not carved, were often painted. The Tahitian canoes were carved on stern and sometimes bow, into small naturalistic figures, sometimes arranged one above the other (the whole series only partially unified). Sometimes only one small bird figure surmounted the long, disproportionately slender stern, which rose nearly perpendicularly from the canoe. The Samoan canoes were sparsely carved on the forward and rear decks, and on the upper side planks. The carving consisted of simple series of deep incisions, triangular in cross sections, incised parallel lines, or rows of interlocking triangles. The most characteristic Samoan canoe decorations were rows of white shells, attached to the tops of the decks.

The temporary decorations varied less. Streamers of tapa were used in Hawaii, the Marquesas and Tahiti; cocoa-nut fronds were used in the Marquesas, and fern fronds in New Zealand. Ropes, strung with tufts of feathers, and tufts of feathers inserted under the battens which covered the seams, were used in New Zealand and the Marquesas. Red feathers were used on the sacred canoes in Tahiti. Human hair and skulls were peculiar to the Marquesas, the antennae-like wands used at the bow, to the Maori canoes[1]. The antennae on Maori canoes are apparently derived from the fishing rods fitted in the same position in Tahitian canoes.

---

[1] A drawing of a canoe from the Island of Mentawei pictured by Rosenberg. Inter. Arch. für Eth. I, 1888, shows similar antennae, and in its whole form and decoration is more like the Maori canoe than the canoes of any of the neighboring groups.

THE HOUSE BUILDING COMPLEX[1]

DESCRIPTION

House Building in Hawaii[2]. — The typical Hawaiian house was a grass house — a light wooden framework completely thatched with grass[3]. The form varied from the house with eaves resting on the ground through the roof whose eaves rested on side-posts, to a hipped roof[4]. Stone houses were sometimes used[5], and on Lanai these house platforms had two divisions, sometimes distinguished only by different qualities of stone work, but sometimes the finely paved portion is six or eight inches higher than the other[6]. The floor was paved with small pebbles and covered with several layers of mats[7]; in the poorer houses the mats were placed over beaten earth, covered with dry grass[8]. The fireplace, which was usually situated[9] in the center of the house, was a slight excavation walled in with flat stones. On Lanai[10], these stones formed a box-like square two feet on a side, often resting on a stone slab. The ridge pole[11] of the Hawaiian house rested on two end-posts which were notched to receive it. This ridge pole was often shorter than the distance between the bases of the two posts, and the posts accordingly slanted inwards. The front and back posts, of which the corner ones were often the stoutest, were grooved to receive the wall plate. Rafters which equalled in number the front and back posts, had their lower ends cut into a heel and fork. The upper ends of the rafters intersected over the ridge pole, and the supplementary ridge pole was placed in the crotch; all four parts were lashed firmly to-

---

[1] As temples were absent in two of the groups, Samoa and New Zealand, the type of construction and consecration ceremonies connected with temples will not be discussed in this paper. For discussion of this feature of Polynesian culture, see Handy, J. P. S., Vol. 35, p. 47.

[2] The earlier data on Hawaiian houses were taken in most cases from the island of Oahu itself. Mr. Emory's recent investigations on Lanai provide new evidence which it is difficult to interpret, as there is not enough information on the amount of variation found throughout the Hawaiian group. Therefore all information referring to Lanai will be so indicated.

[3] Brigham, pp. 267—8. Malo, pp. 159—160.
[4] Brigham, p. 272.
[5] Brigham, p. 274.
[6] Emory, p. 44.
[7] Brigham, p. 308.
[8] Brigham, p. 284.
[9] Brigham, p. 298.
[10] Emory, p. 45.
[11] Brigham, pp. 275—279.

gether. The framework was completed by a lattice of small poles, which were tied from pole to pole at intervals of from five to seven inches. In large houses these were supplemented by vertical poles and cross beams on the roof. The entire house was covered with this lattice work, except the space left for the door. The thatching consisted of a lining of banana leaves, stalks of dried sugar cane or pandanus leaves. The outer thatch consisted of bunches of long grass, placed against the lattice with the roots up, and tied to the rafters with one twist of cord. The thatcher started at the ground and worked up. Several methods were employed in bonneting the ridge-pole, the commonest being either a trimming of grass and ferns, or by braiding the "half of grass on each side with a stiffening of fresh grass, making the bonnet look like a protuberant roll." The thatching of roof and gable walls at the point of intersection presented a most difficult problem, as the Hawaiian house had no projecting eaves. These seams were heavily braided or bonneted with fern fronds, or thicker grass. Around the door space the grass was carefully braided[1]. The form of the door itself is in some doubt[2], but Malo[3] says the top and bottom pieces were rabetted along the edge and that these slid in grooves above and below. The door seems to have been constructed of several transverse pieces, probably grooved together, and secured with cord[4]. The Hawaiians used a bar to fasten the door from within. Some houses contained a veranda, formed either by extensions of the rafters at a slightly reduced slope, or constructed separately in front of the house. When constructed separately this veranda had a flat roof; the roof and side walls were covered with cocoa-nut leaves or tapa[5]. Houses were occasionally raised on posts in regions where floods occurred, and in the absence of flood waters the family resided in the space under the posts[6]. Garrets with a lattice-work floor were sometimes constructed and used as store houses[7]. The houses were surrounded by fences, usually placed very close to the house. These fences were built of palings, or occasionally of stone[8]. On Lanai[9] none of the enclosing walls were high enough to keep out pigs.

In size the average house is described by Stewart[10] as being about eight to ten feet long, six to eight feet broad, and four to six feet high. Houses of chiefs were sometimes 40 to 60 feet long, 20 to

---

[1] Brigham, pp. 280—283.
[2] Brigham, p. 283.
[3] Malo, page 160; Emerson translates this *slide* while Brigham claims the translation should be *swing*. But as his argument is based on false ethnological theory rather than linguistic evidence, it may be disregarded.
[4] Brigham, pp. 280—283.
[5] Brigham, p. 289.
[6] Brigham, p. 272.
[7] Malo, p. 165 (Emerson).
[8] Malo, p. 160; Brigham, p. 101; Corney, p. 90.
[9] Emory, p. 45.
[10] Stewart: *Hawaiian Islands*, p. 182.

25 feet broad, and 18 to 20 feet high[1], while in some parts of the islands Stewart reports huts no higher than his waist[2]. Emory's[3] estimates of house sites on Lanai average 12 feet wide by 20 feet long[4].

The houses of the Hawaiians were highly specialized within the household, varying from a respectable minimum of five to a larger number. There were separate eating houses and separate working houses for men and women; the woman had a special house for withdrawal during menstruation; and there was usually a *heiau*, or house of worship[5]. Canoe houses seem to have been private in the case of fishermen[6], but also to have occurred as communal structures. Brigham's list[7] of housewords[8] gives a special term for council-chamber and for store-house. Malo[9] also mentions large meeting houses, but we have no other records of the storehouse.

The site of the house was usually selected by a divining priest[10]. The future owner and his friends went to the mountains and felled the necessary timber[11]. The front corner posts were the first to be erected. The Hawaiians did not know the method used by the Maori of squaring the house plan by measuring the diagonals[12]; the only device of this kind which they used consisted of stretching a cord across the front posts from end post to end post, to ensure their being of the same height, and halving a cord stretched from front corner posts to rear corner posts, to find the midpoint for placing the post to support the ridge pole. After the initial framework was lashed together, stout cords were bound about this frame, and these were released after the lathes had been tied on, tightening the whole frame by the resulting expansion[13]. The Hawaiians used a net to cover the newly thatched house, so that the grass would dry evenly[14]. If the divining priest had not approved the house site before the house was started, he would do so at its completion[15], after which the consecrating ceremony was performed[16], and the house was then habitable. There were no organized guilds of carpenters

---

[1] Stewart: *Hawaiian Islands*, p. 137.
[2] Ibid., p. 152.
[3] Emory, p. 45.
[4] He could not discover how much of this platform was actually occupied by the house.
[5] Brigham, p. 263; Malo, pp. 50—51 and p. 164.
[6] Brigham, p. 263.
[7] Brigham, p. 302; Emory, p. 51.
[8] Page 302.
[9] Page 185.
[10] Fornander, Series III, p. 58.
[11] Malo, pp. 158—159.
[12] Brigham, p. 275; Best, *The Maori Race*, Vol. II, p. 562.
[13] Ibid., p. 279.
[14] Brigham, p. 283;
[15] Fornander, III, p. 58.
[16] Brigham, p. 287.

in Hawaii[1]. The large houses of the chiefs were built by a system of corvé, the skilled work being done by some of the retainers[2]. The common houses were built by the future owners and their friends[3], and each village contained one or two men more skilled than the rest[4]. These more skilful individuals were called in to plan the framework, and to finish the edges of the roof, the ridge pole, and the corners. There is no record of the time or kind of payment[5]. Final approval of the work rested with the priesthood[6], and united skill in house building and divining powers do not seem to have ever been combined in one person.

The function of the priest consisted of divination of a suitable site[7], or condemnation of a house unsuitably situated or unsatisfactorily constructed (and the cleansing of a house so condemned, by fire and elaborate offerings of plants, fowl, and fish)[8]. Furthermore the priest was sometimes required to sleep in a new house[9], to exorcise evil spirits. But his most important function was in the performance of the consecration ceremony, ("cutting the navel cord of the house"[10]). A special tuft of thatch was left over the door and the priest stood in the doorway, — the owner and his friends standing without, — holding a stone adze in one hand and a tapabeater in the other, recited the *pule* and severed the grass tuft with the adze. It is not clear whether the priest who recited this prayer and the divining priest were the same person or not[11].

The only other rites connected with house building were the occasional human sacrifices which were buried beneath one of the house posts[12]. Hogs were sacrificed to the gods of the priesthood at the ceremony of purifying a condemned house[13].

The chief taboos connected with houses were the mutual taboos preventing men and women from entering each other's eating houses[14]. The woman's house of retirement was also tabooed to men;

---

[1] Brigham, p. 268.
[2] Laurence, p. 71.
[3] Ellis, *Journal*, p. 239.
[4] Laurence, p. 73; Brigham, p. 279. Brigham, p. 265, the great similarity in the interspaces and timber sizes all over the group, which he believed indicated a strictly prescribed procedure.
[5] Laurence, p. 73, says: "They were paid in advance with presents."
[6] Fornander, III, p. 58.
[7] Fornander, III, pp. 58—64.
[8] Ibid., p. 282.
[9] Jarves, p. 42; Brigham, p. 287.
[10] Malo, p. 160; Brigham, p. 287.
[11] Malo, p. 160, refers to the ceremonial priest specifically as the *kahuna pule*.
[12] Brigham, p. 275; Malo, pp. 211—212, mentions that in the sacrifices for one of the special forms of worship followed by the king a "lawbreaker was always chosen as the sacrifice".
[13] Brigham, p. 282.
[14] Eveleth, p. 87; Malo, p. 64; Stewart, C. S., op. cit. contradicts the mutuality of the taboo, but his evidence is not convincing.

the houses of chiefs were tabooed to women and commoners[1]. Stewart[2] also mentions the custom of putting a taboo on a chief's new house by which entrance was prevented except on the payment of gifts. The protective taboo was signified by heavy poles crossed over the door[3], or by a stick with white tapa at the end of it.

Rank seems to have been indicated more by the size and quality of the houses than by any differences in form or decoration[4]. Houses of chiefs were built by a general levy, and taxes were remitted to tenants who provided specially fine timber or grass[5]. Houses of sacred chiefs were taboo, and even the adjoining ground was sacred[6]. Jarves[7] speaks of carved houses, but this does not seem to have been a usual practice. The usual ornamentation consisted of excellence of woodworking[8] and ornamental sennit lashing. The lashings on the houses in the Bishop Museum show very simple patterns[9].

House Building in the Marquesas[10]: — The impression made on early travelers by the Marquesan houses was not a favorable one; they are described as being much inferior to the houses of the Society Islanders[11]. Linton distinguishes between two types: the dwelling-house type, and the small temporary shelter type[12]. The most characteristic feature of the dwelling house of the Marquesas was the sharp pitch of the rear roof which sloped straight to the ground, as contrasted with the short front roof, raised on posts[13]. These houses were always built on stone platforms; the small houses, on the other hand, had no platforms, and were constructed by placing a ridge pole which was triangular in cross sections, on two supporting posts, and leaning rafters on each side from the ridge pole to the ground. This type of house was used for temporary purposes[12].

The platform of the Marquesan house was an essential part of the construction. If the houses were built on a slope, the back edge of the platform was not raised above the level of the ground[14]. It was sometimes ten feet high, usually less than six. This platform was rectangular in shape and divided lengthwise into two unequal

---

[1] Stewart, p. 241 (Hawaiian Islands); Malo, pp. 80—81.
[2] Ibid., p. 103.
[3] Brigham, Figure 86, p. 284.
[4] Ellis, pp. 238—239; Stewart, *Hawaiian Islands*, p. 137.
[5] Brigham, p. 271.
[6] Malo, pp. 80—81.
[7] Jarves, *History of the Hawaiian Islands*, p. 41.
[8] Brigham, p. 274.
[9] Greiner, p. 35, says one pattern used in the sennit lashings is like the oval design found in the Marquesas, the other resembles twilling.
[10] See page 18.
[11] Forster, G., II, p. 21; Cook, I, p. 461.
[12] Page 271.
[13] Handy, p. 153.
[14] This same arrangement occurs on the island of Lanai. Emory, p. 44.

parts, the front section being about twenty inches lower than the rear[1]. A strip of the rear of the house floor was left unpaved, and filled in with soft earth to form the bed space[2]. The front of the platform was faced with large rectangular stone slabs. Circular pits were sometimes left in this platform which extended down to the ground. Sloping stone slabs, serving as back rests, were occasionally built into the veranda portion of the platform[3]. The essential elements of the framework[4], were the end posts upon which rested a ridge pole, the front posts and the stringer[5]. The endposts were usually triangular in cross section and planted six or eight inches within the end of the house wall. They averaged about 13 feet in height. The ridge pole was hewn from a single log, and projected a little at each end of the house. It rested in notches cut in the tops of the end posts, but was not attached in any way. The front posts which were usually three to five feet high were either notched at the top, furnished with a neck which fitted into the front stringer, or left flat[6]. These front posts were usually six in number, but sometimes four or eight. The center pair were placed close together and served as door jambs. Posts were either inserted in holes left in the platform[6], or kept in place by a deeply notched base stringer. The stringer which rested on the top of the front post was either a round pole, or L shaped, resting in notches and lashed to the posts with sennit attachments, which were invisible on the outside and ornamentally elaborated on the inside. The front roof was peculiar in that there were no heavy rafters at the ends. It was constructed of three heavy rafters, one in the middle and the other two half way from each end. Their upper ends rested against the ridge pole, and their lower ends on the stringer. These main rafters were supplemented by additional light rafters of bamboo or peeled *fau* poles, which extended below the stringer, forming eaves, and projected above the ridge pole, forming a crotch where they met the small rafters of the rear roof. The rear roof was supported by eight main rafters, extending from the ridge pole to the ground. The supplementary ridge pole[7] rested in the intersection of the small rafters of rear and front roof. These light rafters were held in place by three horizontal poles, which were lashed securely by sennit or bark string. Both the front and rear roofs extended from six inches to a foot beyond the walls of the house. The walls of the Marquesan house were sometimes lacking entirely, and were usually removable. The end walls were formed of light poles, arranged like an inverted fan, and regularly

[1] Linton, pp. 272—273.
[2] Ibid., p. 282.
[3] Ibid., pp. 272, 273.
[4] Ibid., p. 275, quotes Garcia, who states that formerly center posts were used to support the ridge pole when the two end posts were not sufficient.
[5] Ibid., pp. 275—279.
[6] Linton believes this was the ancient type.
[7] Linton, p. 280.

thatched, or else of pieces of light bamboo, lashed to these uprights. Although the front walls were occasionally thatched, more often they consisted of separate panels, of light poles, corded together and placed between the front posts. These panels were strengthened by cross pieces at the back, which fitted into notches cut in the sides of the front posts. The doorway[1], which was only two to three feet high was placed in the middle of the front of the house, two front posts serving as door jambs, and the stringer sometimes served as a lintel, — occasionally a separate lintel was added. This doorway was closed either by tying together two cocoa-nut leaf mats, one of which was tied to each side post, or by two wooden slabs which slid between additional posts placed just behind the door posts, forming a double-leaf sliding door.

There were no fireplaces in the Marquesan dwelling house[2]. The roof and occasionally the end walls also were thatched with mats eight to twelve feet long, and twelve to eighteen inches wide. These mats were made by "splitting a cocoa-nut frond down the mid-rib, and interweaving the leaflets of either half to form a long narrow mat of checkerboard pattern." These mats were placed on the roof with the mid-rib edge up, and tied to every third or fourth rafter; sennit or bark string was used. The thatch was laid on in tiers, the bottom one being laid on first, and over-lapping heavily, only two or three inches being exposed. Thatching material was also made by stringing the leaves of the bread-fruit tree on long reeds, and from palmetto leaves, so strung on light rods as to give the appearance of shingles. The ridge pole was bonneted[3], either by tying several layers of cocoa-nut mats over the supplementary ridge pole, and securing these by wooden splints, inserted between the two ridge poles, or occasionally by a layer of pandanus leaves placed over the main ridge pole and secured by additional poles placed in the angles made by the intersections of the small rafters. Handy's drawing[4] shows the projection of the front roof beyond the front walls to form a covered veranda running the length of the house.

The bed[3] was an integral part of the house. The rear part of the house floor was covered with soft earth, with its entire surface six to eight inches below the level of the front floor. This space was bordered by dressed palm logs, filled in with fern fronds, and covered with several thicknesses of mats. A bed of intersecting poles, supported on posts eighteen inches to two feet high, is reported for the fishermen's houses at Pua Ma'u, Hiva Oa[5].

---

[1] Linton, p. 282.
[2] Linton, Personal correspondence.
[3] Linton, p. 282.
[4] Handy, *Native Culture in the Marquesas*, p. 153.
[5] Linton, p. 283. On page 282 he quotes Krustenstern and Garcia as mentioning temporary partitions. Brigham, p. 308, reports a mat structure, sometimes extending the length of the room, and occasionally raised on a platform, which he believed was a modern feature.

The household in the Marquesas always consisted of at least two houses, the dwelling house described above, and the cook house[1], which was a shed placed on the ground, thatched with cocoanut leaf mats, and sometimes closed on two or three sides. The oven was a hole in the floor of this shed. In addition there were sometimes a taboo house for men[2], which consisted of a frame raised on posts five to twelve feet high and fifteen to twenty feet square. On this frame work a house was erected. This structure was situated near the dwelling house. There was also a family sacred place, either a small enclosure, or a small high platform on which the temporary houses used at birth[3] and death[4] ceremonies were erected. The chief's establishment contained a house for warriors and a canoe house[5]. These canoe houses seem to have been formed by connecting two heavy posts of equal height with a convex beam, from the center of which rafters ran to the peak of the roof, supporting the ridge pole[6]. Houses erected for tattooing of women and commoners, and for camping were of the temporary small house variety[7]. Houses raised on poles were built for the instruction of young people, as taboo dwellings for men, and store-houses for the food of taboo individuals, and as gathering places for the men to assemble to sing sacred chants[5]. The large sacred structures were of the dwelling type, but with a much higher roof, — their posts being made of several pieces of lumber spliced together[8]. These had three front posts and the front was open. The construction[9] of a house and platform was looked upon as one operation, although new houses were often built on old platforms. Although the house itself was not taboo, the workers were. They had to purify themselves before and after the building operations. The master builder laid the corner-stone of the platform and supervised the construction. A ceremonial "feast of entrance" freed the house for occupancy.

The master builder only supervised the work, leaving most of the labor to the relatives of the owner[5]. The owner fed the workers during the operation. A feast was given at the beginning of the work, and all who came were expected to bring stones[9]. Special craftsmen were employed to put on the ornamental sennit lashings, and to carve the front and end posts. The supervising *tuhuna* was a master craftsman and not a priest[5].

It was the duty of the ceremonial priest to recite the *Pu'e* chant after the corner-stones had been laid, which ended the work for the

---

[1] Handy, p. 64.
[2] Ibid., p. 63.
[3] Ibid., p. 66.
[4] Langsdorf, p. 128.
[5] Linton, p. 271.
[6] Ibid., p. 295.
[7] See page 47.
[8] Linton, p. 295.
[9] Handy, pp. 150—151.

first day. He recited the chant again at the completion of the house. No details are available concerning the "feast of entrance", except[1] a ceremonial by which the mana of the "oracle house" was tested by a body of warriors hurling their spears at the decorated ridge of the new house. This suggests the Maori custom[2] of strangers hurling their spears at a partly completed canoe as a means of divining its future luck.

Sacrifices were offered at the consecration of a chief's house[3]. The temporary houses used for birth were burned[4]. A special house was erected on the second day after the death of a chief, and this house was elaborately decorated. The houses elevated on poles were used as the sleeping houses of taboo men, especially of old men who no longer had any connection with women[5]. These were also used as storehouses for food of taboo men, and as places where men ate taboo food[6]. Stewart[7] says women's houses were not taboo to men. Men and women ate together[8] as a rule. The men engaged in house building had to be purified by bathing[9]. Special houses were erected for taboo occasions like birth and death[10]. The mats on the front of the bed were taboo to men[11]. Only cocoa-nut mats were used on the beds of priests and fishermen, and special raised beds were constructed for priests on which they slept after they had eaten of the sacrifice[11].

The establishment of the chief[12] was the community center, and contained an elaborate dwelling (the posts of which were often carved into human figures[13]), a cook house, store houses, dwellings of attendants, all on stone platforms, warriors' house on a stone platform, and a paved dance space. Here canoe houses were sometimes erected. There was also a carved stone basin in which the chief's eldest son bathed. Special houses were erected for the tattooing of the chief's son[14].

The decoration of Marquesan houses was of three types: ornamental stone work, which might be simple ornamental masonry, figures, carved in high relief on the facing of the platforms, or small

---

[1] Handy, pp. 150—151.
[2] Best, *The Maori Canoe*, p. 48.
[3] Handy, p. 241 quotes Père Siméon, who says human sacrifices were used to remove taboo from a house.
[4] Handy, p. 72.
[5] Ibid., p. 63.
[6] Langsdorf, p. 128.
[7] Stewart, C. S., *A Visit to the South Seas*, p. 241.
[8] Handy, p. 135.
[9] Ibid., p. 150.
[10] Ibid., pp. 72 and 107.
[11] Linton, p. 283.
[12] Handy, p. 40.
[13] Linton, p. 286.
[14] Langsdorf, p. 119; Linton, p. 274, quotes Petit-Thours who says there were raised platforms in the house reserved for the chiefs.

stone statues[1]; carving, and ornamental sennit work. Two distinct methods were employed in the carving, the posts were either carved into human figures or decorated with non-naturalistic conventional designs. The end and front post of most ceremonial buildings and chiefs' houses were carved to represent the human figure. (The carving on the end post usually faced inward.) The heads of these figures were cylindrical, with faces carved in low relief, and finished at the top with a narrow horizontal band, above which a cylindrical neck projected to support the ridge pole or stringer. The bodies and legs of the figures on the end posts were considerably elongated.[2]

The non-naturalistic designs[3] were lightly incised on the flat surfaces, — the outer and inner sides of the front posts, the inside only of end posts. No two posts were identical, but a similarity of motif was observed throughout; both curvilinear and angular geometric designs, applied in horizontal zones of varying width, were used. When the two surfaces of the other sides of the end post were occasionally decorated, they were treated as separate units.

Ornamental lashings[4] of a flat three-strand sennit were used to attach the front post to the stringer, and all the posts to the rafters. These lashings[5] were red, and brown, and black (perhaps yellow and white)[6]. The designs were originated from string figures, by a special *tuhuna*. The houses were not painted[7]. Storehouses were elaborately decorated, sometimes with caryatid figures[8]. Houses were decorated on ceremonial occasions, with tapa streamers and peeled hibiscus poles. Pig skulls were often hung up inside the house[9].

Maori House Building[10]. — Maori houses present a strong contrast between the elaborate houses of assembly, which were beautifully constructed and highly decorated; the *whare puni*, a well built but slightly decorated house; and the dwelling huts constructed of poles and thatch in which the people, sometimes even the chiefs for whom the great houses were built, lived[11]. The essentials of the frame work, however, were the same for all these houses, except that in the

---

[1] Linton, p. 284; the ornamental masonry was confined to Nuka Hiva.
[2] Ibid., p. 286; Pl. xli.
[3] Ibid., p. 287.
[4] Ibid., p. 290.
[5] Ibid., p. 290.
[6] Stewart, *A Visit to the South Seas*, p. 336.
[7] Linton, p. 293.
[8] Linton, Personal correspondence.
[9] Linton, p. 284.
[10] As Herbert Williams' account is incorporated in Hamilton, the page references are all to Hamilton. This section was written before the publication of "The Maori", and the author has not seen the Dominion Bulletin on *The Maori Pa*.
[11] Best, *The Maori*, Vol. II, p. 560; Cook, I, pp. 191—197; Polack, I, pp. 705—708.

poorer ones the broad barge boards[1] were sometimes[2], but not always[3], missing. The window, placed beside the door, seems to have been present in even the smallest houses[2]. The ground plan was oblong, the ends gabled, the sides low under the projecting eaves. The low doorway and window aperture opened out into a veranda[4]. On the Taranaki Coast, Hamilton[5] reports side doors and a side veranda, running the length of the house[6]. The smallest huts were eight to ten feet long and five to eight feet high. The ridge pole was attached to or inserted in two end posts, forked to receive it[7]. Small sticks were fastened to the frame with flax withes from the sides; over these was laid a covering of rushes and an outer thatching of spear grass. The better class of these houses were lined with bark[8], and some of them were sunk a foot or two below the surface-level of the ground[9]. The roof, which sloped in an angle of between thirty and forty-five degrees, projected in front to form a veranda, and was thatched with grass, over which light poles were placed to keep the thatch[3] in place. These small houses contained fireplaces also[7]. Indeed, there were no distinctions between these houses and the great carved houses, except in size, choice of materials, and decorations. Still ruder huts, only thatched on the windward sides, were used by travelers. The cook house, which was sometimes built in conjunction with several others, so that three or four were sheltered by one roof, (although each had its separate entrance[10]), were often constructed of tree-fern trunks[11]. They were built by stretching a flat rush roof over four poles about five feet high[12]. Circular houses were used as cooking houses in some places[13]. Canoe houses were longer and sometimes presented a vaulted appearance[14]. The ceremonial store-houses were raised on posts; and their small doors were contracted at the top[15]. The model in the American Museum shows a floor of light poles with some little distance between each of the single poles[16]. Store-houses were also made by excavating small caves in the side of a hill; although these were very rude in construction, they sometimes had a carved lintel[17]. Raised platforms

---

[1] Broad boards facing the front of the gable.
[2] Hamilton, p. 99.
[3] Ibid., Plate XXV, Fig. 4.
[4] Best, op. cit. Vol. II, p. 562; Tregear, p. 271.
[5] Hamilton, p. 93.
[6] This appears to be the Marquesan type.
[7] Polack, I, p. 206.
[8] Cook, I, p. 191.
[9] Tregear, p. 277.
[10] Marshall, W. B., p. 213.
[11] Best, *The Maori*, II, p. 578, p. 588; Angas, II, p. 125.
[12] Savage, p. 15.
[13] Best, op. cit. p. 588.
[14] Polack, I, p. 91.
[15] Hamilton, p. 91.
[16] A. M. N. H. Model 80.0/2897.
[17] Hamilton, p. 92.

to contain firewood, fish nets, etc., were built near the cook house[1].

But the main effort and ingenuity of the Maori was expended on the *whare whakairo*, or carved house, which was often built as a memorial of some great event, such as a birth of an heir to the principal chief[2]. These houses varied in height from twelve to twenty feet[3]. The main weight of the ridge pole was borne by two heavy posts, the rear one slightly higher than the front. A central pillar, lighter than the end posts, supported the middle of the ridge pole[4]. These end posts might be either whole trunks of trees or slabs. The ridge pole was about ten feet longer than the house, in cross section an obtuse isosceles triangle, sometimes two or more feet across the base. The ridge pole was kept in place by stout pins driven through either side into the posts, by lashing to sunken eyes, and attachment to the rafters. The subsidiary end posts, which were of such height as to give the roof a pitch of about thirty to forty-five degrees, were graduated to correspond to the slope of the ridge pole. The ground plan of the house was squared by measuring the diagonals[5]. The side posts were really heavy planks, one to three feet wide, and three to nine inches thick, with rabbeted edges, and a semi-circular depression in the top to receive the rafters. They leaned slightly inwards and were buttressed behind by stout pieces of rough timber, which were lashed to eyes in the upper ends of the slabs[6]. The intervals between these slabs were a little wider than the slabs themselves. A slender stringer ran the length of the house and was lashed to notches or holes in each slab. The back slabs were similar to the side slabs, except that they stood upright. Their height was set by a wall plate, a board placed on its edge, which extended from one corner post to the other. Each end slab was lashed to this plate. A skirting board was formed by placing slabs horizontally in the intervals between the side slabs. They were rabbeted to fit flush with these side slabs. The rafters were cut into a tongue to fit the depression in the top of the side slabs, and were securely lashed to them.

Their upper ends were lashed together over the ridge pole, and sometimes supported a supplementary ridge pole. These rafters were flat on the outside and somewhat curved on the inside. Horizontal battens were lashed to the rafters, and a trellis work of reeds covered these. The front of the roof was finished by heavy barge boards, which rested on similar vertical facing boards, placed at the front edge of each side wall. The ends of these barge boards

---

[1] Best, *The Maori*, II, p. 578, p. 588; Angas, II, p. 125.
[2] Hamilton, p. 79.
[3] Best, op. cit., Vol. II, p. 563; Polack, I, p. 205.
[4] Best, op. cit., II, p. 563; Tregear, pp. 271—272.
[5] Best, op. cit., p. 563; Hamilton, pp. 82—84.
[6] Compare the Tahitian method of buttressing the reed sides with blocks of stone, p. 59.

projected beyond the house walls, and were carved in a conventional filigree pattern. The door was seldom more than two feet wide and four feet high. It consisted of a slab of wood about two inches thick, which slid along a grooved threshhold into a recess built into the wall. The threshold was a piece of timber, about twice the width of the door, and about a foot thick. Side jambs rested on this threshold and projected beyond it in each direction to form a molding. Across the top of the carved jambs was a richly carved lintel. The window, about two feet square, was similarly constructed. It was usually so high that a man, sitting, could barely look out. The wall spaces between the side slabs were filled with flax mats, or with reed battens, the horizontal lathes, one-half to an inch wide, were lashed to the vertical reeds with colored grasses[1]. Horizontal battens were laid across the back of these battens to keep them in place. The thatch was of bull-rushes placed over the reed work frame, which was securely lashed to the rafters. Further layers of coarse grass completed the thatch. Horizontal poles kept the thatch in place, and sometimes several of these were placed one above the other in different layers[2]. Vines and thick ropes were also used for this purpose[3]. The ridge pole was bonnetted by a row of fern fronds, or by a thick bundle of long grass, bound over the rear end of the ridge pole and securely lashed to the ridge pole and rafters[2]. As Maori houses were not built on stone foundations the floor was simply beaten earth, strewn with rushes and ferns.[4] The bed spaces on either side of the door were marked off by planks pegged to the floor, and filled with fern-fronds[5]. The fireplace was a hollow square enclosed either by a row of stones or by wood[6]. Each family group[7] of houses was sometimes surrounded by a fence, made with posts inserted in the ground, to which horizontal rails were securely lashed. The whole village[8] was sometimes surrounded by a large fence of this character, with periodic large posts, carved to represent defiant warriors. The smaller posts were notched at the top, so as to resemble human heads[9]. A great variety of forms of barricades and excavated earthworks[10] were used.

The functional division of houses was within the village group, rather than within the household; even the individual cook houses

---

[1] Hamilton, p. 85; Tregear, p. 272; Best, *The Maori*, II, p. 567.
[2] A. M. N. H. Model 80.0/2897.
[3] Hamilton, p. 85.
[4] Ibid., p. 87.
[5] Polack, I, pp. 165—166.
[6] Cook, I, p. 191.
[7] Best, *The Maori*, Vol. II, p. 335; Buller, p. 233; Hamilton, p. 72.
[8] A detailed mention of the Maori fortifications is omitted as there is no comparative material from some other parts of Polynesia. Best, op. cit., p. 304.
[9] Best, op. cit., Vol. II, p. 324; Hamilton, Plate XXV, Fig. 4.
[10] Colenso, T. N. Z. I., Vol. I, p. 350; Best, op. cit., Vol. 2, chap. 15, passim.

sometimes being united in groups[1]. The great carved houses were sometimes divided into council chambers, sacred houses for the instruction of the young men, guest houses[2], and houses where the whole tribe slept in time of war[3]. Store-houses were highly decorated and extremely taboo[4]. Special huts were erected for the initiation of the chief's son into the priesthood[5], and for the birth of a child of rank[6]. But a large number of specialized houses within the household establishment does not seem to have occurred, although chiefs had separate houses for their respective wives[7]. Store houses were tribal, the possession of the chief, or sometimes individual in the case of the rough, half-sunken house. Crozet[8] mentions three tribal store-houses, for arms, food, and nets.

The materials for a new house were often collected months before, as the bull-rushes had to be cut in the month of March, and the reeds carefully prepared. The ground was first leveled by the eye, and the builders then waited for the first rain, to show up depressions[9].

There were parts of the work which according to Polack[10] were done by the chiefs. Slaves and chiefs[11] worked together on the same house. Carving was specialized tribally, and must have set the same premium on natural skill as in the case of canoe building. The chiefs directed the work of the party which went out to select timber[12].

The priest divined the time for commencing operations[13], and performed "appropriate ceremonies", and recited "proper *Karakias*" (chants) before its erection[14]. He also performed the consecration ceremony. In this ceremony the priest tied a sacred plant to the back center post, and held a bundle of sacred shrubs in his hand. The charms[15] followed a definite order, the first to propitiate Tane; the second, at which the priest ascended the roof[16], was to remove the taboo from the carver's sacred instruments[17], and the wood carved into images of the gods. It was at this stage that the priest struck the various carvings of the house with the shrub which he held

[1] Marshall, p. 213.
[2] Tregear, p. 271.
[3] Colenso, T. N. Z., Vol. I, p. 350; Best, *The Maori*, Vol. 2, chap. 15, passim.
[4] Hamilton, p. 92; Best, op. cit., Vol. II, p. 587.
[5] Tregear, J. R. A. I., Vol. xix, p. 99.
[6] Tregear, *The Maori Race*, p. 27.
[7] Colenso, T. N. Z. I., Vol. I, p. 350.
[8] Quoted by Hamilton, p. 91.
[9] Williams, H. P., J. P. S. Vol. v, pp. 145—154.
[10] Vol. I, p. 205.
[11] T. N. Z. I., Vol. xii, p. 116.
[12] Polack, I, p. 168.
[13] Williams, p. 145.
[14] Hamilton, p. 80, no details supplied; Best, op. cit., Vol. II, p. 587.
[15] Cowan, pp. 173—176; Best, op. cit., Vol. II, p. 575.
[16] Tregear, pp. 278—279.
[17] All the tools of the workers were placed above the barge boards.

in his hand. The third incantation was an appeal to the gods to make the house warm. The whole ceremony was known as "binding the *maro* of the house." The priest then entered the house[1] by a window and opened the door. The threshold was first crossed by three women of rank, so that food might be brought into the house[2], and to keep the ridge pole from sagging[1]. Human sacrifices[3] were sometimes offered at the building of a great house, or the fence of an important *pa*. In the latter case a slave was buried under one of the posts[4]. In the former[1], a member of the tribe was killed, sometimes the favorite child of the chief, the heart was cut out and eaten, and the body buried beneath one of the posts. The particular post selected varied from tribe to tribe. Occasionally a distinguished captive was so sacrificed.

The whole operation of building was taboo, no woman might enter the new house, and it was taboo to cook food on a fire made from chips from the sacred house carvings[5]. Sacred chiefs' houses were taboo[5], and any house which he entered became taboo[6]. Chiefs' store-houses and *kumara* store-houses were taboo[7]. It was taboo to lean against the wall of a house[8] and the inner threshhold was taboo[9]. Elaborate knots to secure the door seem to have been substituted for the protective taboo[10]. Food was never taken into the sacred houses[11], and usually not into dwellings[12]. Chiefs were forced to eat in the open air[13], for fear of tabooing a house. *Kumara* storehouses were especially sacred[14], and if a chief's shadow fell on a food store[15], it had to be destroyed. If by accident food was cooked on a fire made from sacred chips, food cooked on similar chips could be eaten by a woman of rank, and the damage repaired[16]. Chiefs had to repair their own houses as no slaves could venture upon the roof, which had been above a chief's sacred head[17].

The rank of a chief was emphasized more by the fact that he had

---

[1] Tregear, pp. 278—279.
[2] Cowan, p. 179.
[3] Best, *The Maori*, II, p. 576; Best, *Maori Religion and Mythology*, Sec. I, p. 144.
[4] Hamilton, p. 73.
[5] Cowan, pp. 173—176; Best, op. cit., Vol. II, p. 575.
[6] Williams, pp. 145—154.
[7] Tregear, p. 157.
[8] Shortland, *Traditions and Superstitions of the Maori*, p. 112.
[9] Tregear, p. 275.
[10] Ibid., p. 199.
[11] Williams, J. P. S. Vol. v, pp. 145—154.
[12] Hamilton, p. 72.
[13] Tregear, p. 194.
[14] Ibid., p. 157.
[15] Brown, W. p. 14, says this was done for fear some chief might subsequently enter the house.
[16] Tregear, p. 278.
[17] Brown, W., p. 14.

several houses than by the quality of any one of them[1]. The place of honour in a house was under a window[2], while the left hand corner (facing the house) was allotted to the slaves[3]. Slaves were forbidden to approach a *kumara* house[4]; women, however high their rank, could not enter the holy house of learning. Special rafter patterns were used on chief's houses[1], and Cowan[5] says possession of a carved house was one of the three indispensable attributes of rank.

The decoration[6] of the Maori house can be subdivided into carving, rafter painting, and reed work. Sometimes the carving was painted, especially in the case of the heavily carved slabs over the door and window, and in the case of store-houses. When carving did occur in ordinary dwellings it was on the barge-boards, the vertical facing boards, and sometimes on the broad piece of timber which faced the front of the veranda. A carved face was placed over the junction of the barge boards, and occasionally a human figure placed above this. The projecting end of the ridge pole was sometimes carved. Storehouses were carved all over on the outside. Each separate panel of wood was treated as a decorative unit.

The outside was carved as described above, more elaborately in the case of the large houses. In the large houses these slabs were carved on the inside in high relief into conventionalized human figures. A small human figure was carved in the round at the foot of the center pole. The panels in between the side slabs were decorated with reed work in elaborate step and checker patterns. These were occasionally modified in an attempt to approximate to the designs of the slab carvings. The rafters were painted in red and white curvilinear designs. The carving was decorated with inlaid haliotis shell.[7]

The style was characterized as in the case of canoe carving by extensive use of the double scroll, combined with conventionalizations of the human figure, a tendency to intricate incidental decoration and towards treating the part of the object decorated as a unit. House carvings were occasionally decorated with feathers, and shrubs were sometimes planted around them.

House Building In Tahiti. — The typical Tahitian house was oval[8], covering, according to Cook, a space twenty-four feet by eleven feet, according to Wilkes, fifty to sixty by twenty feet. The guest house was sometimes 200 feet long, 30 feet broad, and 20 feet high at the ridge pole[9]. In addition to its oval shape, the most

---

[1] Colenso, T. N. Z. I. Vol. i, pp. 755—757.
[2] Williams, p. 151.
[3] Hamilton, p. 105.
[4] Tregear, p. 157.
[5] Page 163, but this may have been in a tribal sense. See, Polack, II, page 205.
[6] Hamilton, Plates.
[7] Tregear, p. 273.
[8] Cook, I, p. 83; Wilkes, I, p. 142.
[9] Cook, loc. cit.

characteristic feature of the Tahitian house was the extra row of pillars in the center which supported the ridge pole[1]. But this seems to have occured only in the larger houses, as Hugenin's drawing[2] shows instead three strong transverse rafters, on which rest extra posts extending up to the ridge pole. Forster[1] says this middle row of posts contained posts 20 feet high in the large houses, and 8—10 feet in the smaller ones. The smallest houses were almost round, and the longest ones approximated an oblong, rather than an oval. The cook house was oblong, as were the canoe sheds. The ridge pole was about nine inches in diameter, and triangular in cross section; square mortices were made to receive the tenons, forming the tops of the ends posts[3]. Tahitian houses ordinarily had floors of trampled earth[4]. Houses near the sea were sometimes raised on blocks of coral or wooden piles[5], and rectangular stone platforms[6] were sometimes used. Blocks of stone[5] were occasionally put at the foot of the bamboo walls to give them stability. The side posts were placed about three or four feet apart, and grooves six to eight inches in depth and an inch to an inch and a half wide were cut in the top of each post to receive the wall plate, a board eight or nine inches broad, beveled on its upper edge. Hugenin's drawing[2] shows two straight wall pieces extending along the front and back of the house, and curved wall plates, resting on posts of regularly decreasing height, extending around each end. Cook[7] gives the height of the shortest post as three and a half feet, when the ridge pole is nine feet from the ground. The rafters were notched about 18 inches from the end to receive the wall plates[8], thus forming eaves about a foot and a half in extent. Parallel rafters were placed on each side of the roof, a supplementary ridge pole was placed in the intersection and the whole tied firmly together and to pegs inserted in the main ridge pole. The walls of the house[8] were made of light poles, two or three inches in diameter. These were planted about two or three inches apart, in a trench about a foot deep, until the building was completely enclosed except for the door space. Two or three light sticks were tied horizontally on the outside. (Cook[9] says the dwelling house had no walls.) The door[10] was a light trellis frame of bamboo, suspended by a number of braided thongs, from a long cane in the upper part of the inside of the wall plate. These thongs slid back and forth like curtain rings.

---

[1] Forster, G., pp. 455—456.
[2] Page 115.
[3] Ellis, I, p. 384.
[4] Ibid.
[5] Hugenin, p. 117.
[6] Linton, p. 450.
[7] Cook, I, p. 83.
[8] Ellis, I, pp. 384—388; Hugenin, pp. 113—115.
[9] Loc. cit.
[10] Ellis, I, p. 389.

The house was thatched[1] with pandanus leaves, which were doubled "about one-third of the way from the stalk, over a strong reed or cane, about six feet long, and the folded leaf laced together with the stiff stalks of the cocoa-nut leaflets." These were sewn to cords stretched from rafter to rafter and each series of three was firmly bound to the rafters with sennit. The ridge pole was bonnetted by placing a row of large cocoa-nut or fern leaves along the ridge, and weaving in a species of long grass. Hugenin's[2] figure of a house raised on posts, shows a veranda similar to that found in the Marquesas, but as this house has a plank floor, this may be due to European influence. Every chief's house was surrounded by a fence, about four feet high, constructed of upright sticks, surmounted by a polished rail[1]. The court yard was paved with black basalt pebbles or ground coral. The floor of beaten earth was covered with long dry grass or mats[3]. Wilkes[4] speaks of cane bed-steads and occasional screens of tapa. Cook describes the small portable houses which were used as sleeping houses by the chiefs, and carried from place to place on the canoe. The cook house[5] was a simple rectangular structure. In the canoe house the rafters and side poles were formed of one piece, giving a vaulted effect[6]. These were occasionally used as dwelling houses. Forster[7] mentions small houses shaped like hurdles erected within the house. Houses for childbirth were of this nature[8]. Although information is not very specific, there seem to have been eating houses for men and women[9]. Moerenhout mentions a special house for tapa making[10]. An important feature of the Tahitian village was the guest house, which was used as a place of assembly also; and was capable of holding several hundred people[11]. In this house the members of the *Areois* Society were accommodated, and there they gave their dramatic performances. Wilson[12] suggests the presence of several guest houses in a village, for the accommodation of individual visitors of rank. Ellis describes one of these guest houses in Pare, which was 397 feet long, and belonged to the king. These great houses are reported to have had a long enclosure at one side[13].

---

[1] Ellis, I, p. 389.
[2] Page 18.
  Wilson, p. 331; Cook, I, p. 83, says that the floor was covered six inches
[3] deep with mats, and that there were no special bed places.
[4] Vol. I, p. 342; this is probably a modern development.
[5] Hugenin, p. 114.
[6] Parkinson, Pl. xii.
[7] Page 465.
[8] Wilson, p. 341.
[9] Ellis, I, p. 222; Wilson, p. 331.
[10] Vol. II, p. 92.
[11] Cook, I, p. 83; Wilson, p. 350; Ellis, I, p. 388.
[12] Page 350.
[13] Cook, I, p. 83.

There are no records of the procedure of house building in Tahiti except Hugenin's remark[1] that district houses and chief's houses were built by a general levy. This statement corresponds to Wilson's description of canoe building[2].

Our information about craft division is also scanty. Ellis[3] and Moerenhout[4] speak of patron gods of carpenters and of thatchers. Ellis mentions that the difficult tasks in house building were the thatching of the angles and the bonnetting of the ridge poles[5], and that regularly trained men were called in to do this work. Women made the thatching mats[6].

The only priestly function recorded is that of the sacrificing priest who officiated when a new house was built for the king or a temple erected. It was this priest who selected a victim from the assembled crowd[7].

Ellis[8] reports that prayers were offered before building a new house, but gives no details. The houses of chiefs and priests[9] were taboo, and the houses of the men were taboo to the women[10]. A special opening was made in the side of the house through which the food of a new born child was passed, because the food of a child could not enter by the same door as the food of a mother[11].

The houses of the chiefs were built by the tenant class[12], and chief's houses as well as public buildings had special ornamental sennit decorations on the inside of the rafters[13]. Chiefs' houses had high enclosures around them, and paved court yards[3]. Chiefs slept sometimes in small collapsible dwellings, which they took with them on canoe journeys[14].

Nothing is known of the decoration of Tahitian houses, except Ellis's statement[5] that braided sennit cords or finely fringed white or checkered matting decorated the rafters of public buildings and chiefs' houses. These seem to have been streamers which hung down twelve or thirteen inches, a quite different style of decoration from the sennit lashings of Hawaii and the Marquesas.

House Building in Samoa. — There are two forms of Samoan house, — the round house with the roof supported by one to four

---

[1] Page 117.
[2] Page 281.
[3] Ellis, II, pp. 199—200.
[4] Moerenhout, I, p. 452.
[5] Vol. I, p. 386.
[6] Hugenin, p. 113.
[7] Tyerman and Bennett, Vol. II, p. 181; Ellis, II, p. 212.
[8] Vol. II, p. 216.
[9] Moerenhout, I, p. 532.
[10] Ellis, I, p. 271; but Wilson, p. 351, speaks of men and women keeping to different ends of the house when they ate in the same house.
[11] Wilson, p. 351.
[12] Wilson, p. 324; Forster, p. 356.
[13] Ellis, Vol. I, p. 386.
[14] Cook, I p. 83.

strong central posts; and the long house, in which the longer roof is supported by additional lines of heavy pillars inside the house. Both forms have high pitched thatch roofs resting on short pillars four to five feet in height. The house floor is raised eight to twelve inches by a platform of small round stones dressed with carefully chosen bits of coral. In the case of large round houses belonging to chiefs, the house was placed in the center of a series of shallow terraces six or seven inches high, one to three feet wide, and faced with squared coral blocks. The fireplace was built near the center of the house[1]; sometimes there were two fireplaces, one on each side of the center post. It was a circular hollow, lined with hard clay, two or three feet in diameter, and occasionally enclosed with stones.

The basis of the framework[2] of a round house was one to four strong center poles, about twenty-five feet in height, supporting a ridge pole, from which heavy rafters extended to the side posts. These rafters were held in place by rounded beams, lashed on at intervals. These beams were semi-circular at the ends of the house. Small battens, adzed from bread-fruit wood, and jointed together, filled the spaces between the rafters in rows of six. A peculiar feature of the round house was the construction of the roof in such a way that it could be taken apart, usually in three pieces, — the center piece in which the rafters were parallel to each other, and the two ends in which the rafters were curved. These pieces were elevated on the basic three-piece ridge pole frame work and lashed to the lower pole and to each other. When the long house form was used[3], a cross section of the frame-work shows a cross beam resting on rows of high side posts. This beam supported stout uprights on which rested the ridge pole. The Samoan house had no walls as a usual thing, but instead blinds of plaited cocoa-nut leaves were let down between the posts, and rolled up in the day time. Occasionally the sides of the houses were partly walled with mats of bamboo attached to sticks planted upright in the ground and lashed to the eaves[4]. The small temporary house[5], still erected in the bush, had a span roof and the simplest form had only one side, slanting from ridge pole to ground, thatched in. This resembles the small house used on the double canoes[6]. Fishermen's huts were also of the one-sided type. The cookhouse was of the simplest rectangular form[7], square at the ends and thatched with palm leaves.

---

[1] Turner, p. 156; Wilkes, I, p. 100.
[2] Hood, pp. 31—33; Krämer, II, pp. 223, 228; Brown, p. 25; Stair, p. 106.
[3] Stair, p. 106, says the long house was imported from Tonga in recent times. These Tongan houses were oblong with the two ends closed; the roof sloped to pillars about four feet high. See Mariner, II, p. 195. But the Tutuila tradition insists that the round house is the more recent.
[4] Brown, p. 334.
[5] Krämer, II, p. 222.
[6] Ibid., p. 251.
[7] Ibid., p. 223.

The thatch[1] was made by stringing dried sugar cane leaves on pieces of reed about five feet long, and fastening them by "overlapping one end of the leaf, and pinning it with the ribs of the cocoanut leaflet, run through horizontally from leaf to leaf." These mats were three or four feet deep, and each one overlapped the next an inch or two. The thatching was begun at the eaves, and fastened to the inner rafters with sennit; bonnetting was accomplished by broad palm leaf mats[2]. A net work of sennit or more often of cocoa-nut leaves was laid over the thatch to keep it from blowing[3]. The house was occasionally partitioned by curtains of bark cloth, six or eight feet deep. At night mosquito tents of tapa[4] strung on strings of sennit across the end of a house were suspended from the rafters and distended by bent sticks[5]. Houses of chiefs are said to have been surrounded by a high double fence, the outer one of stout posts, and the inner one of reeds. A zigzag entrance, several feet long, penetrated this enclosure[6].

The specialization of houses was not carried to such an extent in Samoa, within the household establishment itself. The great houses[7] which served as guest houses and council chambers, occupied the most important position in the village. A number of the cast-off wives of chiefs were attached to this house for the convenience of travelers[8]. These houses were also used as sleeping places for the young men of the village[9], although sometimes they built themselves an insubstantial house on piles out over the water[10]. Each family had a cooking house attached to the establishment[11]. A chief's establishment contained one large house and several smaller houses for his family and retainers[8]. There were also canoe houses which were very long, triangular in cross-section, and thatched to the ground. Special houses were erected for tattooing. The guest houses of the principal chiefs were located near the village green, the *malae*, while the smaller houses and outhouses were set back from these more pretentious dwellings. Some Samoan villages were surrounded by rough stone walls to keep out the pigs.

The procedure of house building was similar to that of canoe building. The man who wished to have a house built took an initial gift of food to a recognized carpenter. The carpenter, if he wished to take the contract, accepted the food and invited certain lesser craftsmen and young men of his household to eat it with him. This

[1] Turner, pp. 153—154.
[2] Krämer, I, p. 226, Bild 88.
[3] Ibid., p. 237.
[4] Stair, p. 105.
[5] Brown, p. 26.
[6] Ibid.
[7] Wilkes, I, p. 203; Krämer, II, p. 225.
[8] Pritchard, p. 132.
[9] Stair, p. 109—110.
[10] Churchward, p. 319.
[11] Brown, p. 130; Turner, p. 112.

constituted an invitation to help him with the construction of the house. Kava ceremonies, feasts and payments of tapa and fine mats punctuated the construction at regular intervals, culminating in the *Umu Sa*, or "Sacred Oven", when the last payments were made, and all the carpenters in the village came to participate in the festivities. The kava was drunk in the name of the particular god of carpenters, and the courtesy titles of the carpenters were recited. At this ceremony the chief officiating carpenter, whatever his rank in the social structure of the village, had to be addressed with the most extreme courtesy phrases. The *Umu Sa* made a Samoan house socially existent. It had no real religious significance but is analogous functionally to the religious ceremonies in other areas.

At the marriage of a chief, the whole community combined to build the stone platform for his new house[1], which was given as a gift to the bride. Craft lines were more rigid than among the canoe builders[2]. If the workers were not satisfied with the recompense they received, they removed one beam in the roof, making a conspicuous gap which no other worker dared to fill[3].

No religious rites are recorded. Human sacrifices do not appear to have occurred. The taboo eating houses for men and women do not occur, and although a separate cook-house existed, it had lost its significance, for men of rank participated in cooking[4]. The dwelling houses of certain of the highest chiefs were sacred from intrusion[5]. It was taboo to stand up in a canoe, or to carry a lighted torch while passing a chief's house[5]. The rank of a chief was indicated by the size of his principal house[6], the height and number of terraces in the platform, and the number of cross beams which supported the roof as well as by the quality of the wood and the general workmanship. Chiefs' establishments were formerly surrounded by high palisades[7]. A temporary partition was made by placing a partly unrolled upright belt of matting around the spot where the chief slept[8], and certain high chiefs had raised bed places at one end of the house, the main part of the elevation being accomplished by an enormous number of mats. This bed place was faced with two or three strips of bamboo.

The Samoan houses were very little decorated, and the whole artistic emphasis was on beauty of workmanship. The small rafters were sometimes alternately of dark and light shades[9], and the aim of the Samoan craftsman was to make his roof like the rainbow[10].

---

[1] Stair, p. 111; Churchward, p. 320.
[2] Stair, p. 156; Brown, pp. 305—306.
[3] Brown, p. 307.
[4] Turner, p. 112.
[5] Brown, pp. 181—182.
[6] Ibid., p. 25.
[7] Ibid., p. 243.
[8] Stair, p. 111.
[9] Hood, p. 32.
[10] Brown, p. 25.

The only decorations were sennit lashings, an ornamental elaboration of the necessary lashings at the top of each post where it was joined to a rafter and on the cross beams in the center of the house. The principal preoccupation of the artist was to make each lashing a little different from the last. The use of brightly colored lashings[1] and of paint in the vacant spaces to offset the lashed patterns is probably of recent introduction.

ANALYSIS OF HOUSE BUILDING.

The houses have certain basic features in common throughout the five groups. The use of the heavy ridge pole, resting on two or more supporting posts, and the roof, based on rafters running from the ridge pole to the side posts was found throughout the area. Doors, when they occurred, were constructed so as to slide. The bonnetting of the roof was accomplished by using a supplementary ridge pole. Wood was used for the frame work throughout, although in the temporary Maori structures very light reed was used. Lashing was the principal device used in attaching the parts to each other. The small temporary house, triangular in cross section, was very similar in form. The principal variation in the form of the small house was in the choice of material, in which case it then conformed to the prevalent usage of each particular group. Some form of specialization in house building, particularly the thatching of the ridge and some ceremony or taboos occur in all five cultures. The connection with rank is close but highly variable. An aesthetic premium was set upon some aspect of the construction of the house, but important decoration did not occur in all cases.

The variations in the house itself were due to changes in form, rather than to the introduction of any new mechanical principles. Functional changes were few in number. In Hawaii the use of eaves was unknown, and in consequence the Hawaiians had developed an elaborate method of thatching the inner section of roof and walls. The Hawaiian builder bound the basic framework of his house tightly with ropes, and counted on the spring resulting from releasing this tension, to tighten the lashings and give stability to the whole structure. The Hawaiian ridge pole was shorter than the distance between the feet of the end posts, so that the walls slanted inwards. In the Maori house the ridge pole slanted toward the front of the house to let the smoke escape, the side posts were graduated accordingly, and slanted somewhat inward; they were buttressed with extra slabs. In Tahiti the sides of the house were similarly reinforced with blocks of stone. In the Samoan house the lack of permanent walls eliminated the specific door space and door adaptation, while in Tahiti the door was a mat which slid along a horizontal rod like a curtain. The side posts were grooved to receive the rafters.

---

[1] Handy, *Samoan Housebuilding*, pp. 13—14.

5

The veranda was found in Hawaii, — sometimes as a separate structure, — and in the Marquesas and New Zealand, where it was an integral part of the house. Maori houses sometimes had verandas at each end, and for one district side verandas are reported. Real windows occurred only in New Zealand, though appertures for passing in food were left in Tahitian houses. Fireplaces, sunk in the floor, and walled in by stones, were used in dwelling houses everywhere, except in the Marquesas. Houses on piles were used as store houses in New Zealand, as store and ceremonial houses in the Marquesas, as practical shelter against flood in Tahiti and Hawaii, and, built out over the water, served as bachelors' sleeping quarters in Samoa. The methods of thatching varied considerably, principally in response to the available materials, although three separate methods, using as many kinds of material, are reported for the Marquesas. The fabrication of long thatching mats by pinning leaves over long reeds, and the application of these mats to the framework, producing a shingled effect, was similar in Samoa, Tahiti, and the Marquesas. The Maori used the groundwork of reeds, upon which raupo rush thatching was superimposed, and the Hawaiians used grass entirely. A thick bundle of grass was used as the unit. Maori houses were sometimes lined with bark, and Hawaiian with leaves. In Samoa, Hawaii, and Tahiti the ridge was bonnetted by braiding the thatching material with fern fronds, or by mats; in New Zealand long rows of grass were used. Heavy mats were used in Samoa and the Marquesas, — in the latter case these were skewered to the frame with wooden splints. In the construction of the walls there was considerable variation, from the Hawaiian house with its complete covering of thatch, except for the door space, through the partly thatched, partly woven, movable panels of the Marquesan house, the permanent reed walls of Tahiti, the heavily carved paneled Maori house walls, to the use of light mats which rolled up like awnings in Samoa. Platforms of stone were used sometimes in Hawaii, always in the Marquesas, occasionally in Tahiti and Samoa, but have not been recorded in New Zealand. Fences occured frequently in Hawaii, around chiefs' houses in Tahiti, and around groups of houses and also around the whole village in New Zealand.

Aside from the variations in the kind of material used, the greatest diversity was in the form of the house, which had undergone a unique development in each group, although the occurence to the present day of the small temporary house, triangular in cross section, in all the groups seems to suggest a possible unity of original form. The Hawaiians had developed a hipped roof, and this feature, together with the completely thatched walls, served to individualize the Hawaiian house. In the Marquesas the rear roof sloped steeply from ridge pole to ground, while the front roof was raised on short pillars. Among the Maori the Hawaiian type had been modified by the use of wooden planked walls, the broad barge boards facing the gable and the edges of the front walls, the projection of the ridge pole, and the introduction of a window. In Tahiti the houses were oblong with rounded ends, the end posts being graduated in height and lower than the side posts. The walls were of reeds planted in the earth, and the door a mat which slid on a horizontal rod. The Samoan house, although possessing the fundamental structural form of a ridge pole on two or more posts, with rafters extending from it, was round or eliptical in ground plan. The horizontal beams used in the construction of the roof were curved. Still more variety is noticeable in the form of the special houses, such as the cook house, which was triangular in cross section in the Marquesas, rectangular and gabled in Samoa and Tahiti, and flat roofed in New Zealand; or the storehouses on piles which are found in New Zealand, Samoa and the Marquesas.

The amount of division of houses by function varied enormously. The separate cook house is omnipresent, in New Zealand several sometimes being united under one roof, but in Samoa it had quite lost its original segregative purpose as men and even chiefs took part in the cooking, and men and women ate together. The specialization of buildings within the household was most highly developed in Hawaii, where five separate buildings represented the minimum at which respectability could be maintained, and specialization within the village reached its height in New Zealand. Hawaiian houses contained lattice floored garrets, which were used as storehouses; the Marquesans built raised store-houses on piles, in which taboo men ate and slept and boys were ceremonially instructed. In the Maori village these raised storehouses held different types of sacred articles. The Marquesans seem to have had separate houses where the men gathered for ceremonial activities, and they also had a warriors' house in the chief's establishment. The canoe house performed a similar function in Hawaii, while the guest house in Samoa was sometimes used as a bachelors' club house, though occasionally special houses were constructed for this purpose. The use of the guest house was most highly developed in Samoa, where it was the socio-ceremonial center of the village, and in Tahiti and New Zealand. It seems to have been relatively unimportant in Hawaii. The usage in regard to construction of temporary houses for different special occasions varied still more. No special birth houses are recorded even for the birth of children of rank in Hawaii and Samoa; it was used in the other three groups, but erected inside the house in Tahiti. Special houses for tattooing were built in the Marquesas and Samoa, and for the use of the workers on a canoe or house in New Zealand and the Marquesas.

The status of the craftsmen was extremely variable. In Hawaii there were no organized groups of builders, but each village possessed one or two semi-professional carpenters, who knew the specifications for a house and were expert in bonnetting the ridge and performing the other difficult parts of the thatching; but the bulk of the work was done by the future owner and his relatives. In the Marquesas the chief carpenter enjoyed considerable prestige and even performed some of the ceremonies. The heavy work was done by relatives and friends of the future owner under the carpenter's direction. All the workmen were taboo during the operation. The chiefs seem to have exercised considerable executive functions in New Zealand, supervising the cutting of the trees, and even working on the houses themselves. A good deal of the rougher work was done by slaves, and specialization seems to have been more particularly limited to the decoration of the house. In Tahiti the feudal regulations seem to have been in force in the construction of houses of any size. The thatchers and the carpenters were distinct groups, but our information for this aspect of Tahitian culture is too scanty for useful comparisons. As in the case of the canoe builders, the Samoan carpenters enjoyed great power and prestige. Their engagement and payment amounted to a ritual, their emoluments were tremendous. A system of apprenticeship had been developed, and their professional consciousness was articulate to the point of disciplining recalcitrants.

The priests in Hawaii divined the suitability of the house site, and possessed the final veto power upon the finished house. He could be engaged to avert the evil inherent in faulty construction, and this fact makes it somewhat ambiguous as to whether he condemned technical or religious deficiencies in the new structure. He also slept in the new house and performed the consecration ceremony. In the Marquesas, the priest officiated at the beginning and at the completion of a new house, chanting the *Pu'e*, and making offerings. His functions seem to have been concomitant with those of the chief builder and his relation to the "feast of entrance" is not recorded. Among the Maori the priests also divined the house site, recited chants during the progress of the work, and performed the consecration ceremony. But this ceremony was only made complete by the offices of women of rank, who must first "trample the threshold." Furthermore, if any serious infractions of the taboos incident to house building or houses occurred, although the priest performed the routine ceremonial work, the food which was to remove the taboo had to be ceremonially eaten by a woman of rank. In Tahiti the priest officiated in offering the human sacrifices at the building of the king's house, and in Samoa he had no function.

The consecration feast, with a priest officiating, occurred in the Marquesas, Hawaii, and New Zealand, but with different emphasis in the last two cases for which we have details. Among the Maori the stress was laid on the removing of taboos connected with the sacred wood, in freeing the tools and the workers from taboo, and "in binding the sacred *maro* of the house," — i. e., in assuring warmth to the future inmates. In Hawaii the ceremonies were directed against initial evil occupants who were conceived as already in residence, and "in cutting the navel cord" of the new house. In the Marquesas the workers were taboo and had to be consecrated to the labor, but no details are given neither of this nor of the entrance feast.

Human sacrifices were offered in Hawaii, in the Marquesas where they were obtained by organized raids, among the Maori where a chief's child or a distinguished captive was occasionally slain, and in Tahiti where the victim was selected from the assembled crowd. Human sacrifices did not occur in Samoa in connection with house building. The variation was in the type of victim chosen and from this point of view the practices in New Zealand, the Marquesas and Tahiti are distinctly incomparable.

The taboos connected with the building of the house and with the house itself were almost completely variable. Taboo eating-houses for men occurred in Hawaii and the Marquesas, and for men and for women in Hawaii and Tahiti, although this regime was not so strictly enforced in Tahiti. In Hawaii this motive was combined with the tabooed cook house and in New Zealand the cook houses were entered only by women and slaves, while in Samoa the still separate cook house was freely entered by men of all ranks. The need for the segregation of men at certain times, in Hawaii, when engaged in certain activities in the Marquesas, was obtained by taboo houses, but the segregation of the unmarried men in Samoa was a casual and voluntary affair, surrounded with no such sanctities. Storehouses were taboo among the Maori because they contained food, in the Marquesas if they contained the food of tabooed men. The Hawaiian house was protected in the owner's absence by a taboo sign, in New Zealand by ingenious and difficult knots. The threshold and walls of the Maori house were taboo; the mats on the front of the bed were taboo to men in the Marquesas. Examples might be multiplied indefinitely to show how this basic conception of taboo attached itself to any and every aspect of the house in different groups. Removal of taboo was effected in New Zealand by food ceremonies, in Hawaii by sacrificing to the gods of the officiating priesthood.

The connection with rank was immediate and logically determined. In all the groups the chiefs had the ability to possess finer houses than those of the other members of the tribe, either by virtue of the possession of greater wealth or by their claims on communal labor. In Hawaii their houses were better built and more ornamented; and the principal chiefs had carpenters among their retainers. Materials might be requisitioned from the tenants, and they in turn had a lien on the materials on their chief's land. Taxes might also be remitted in return for good materials. In the Marquesas the chief's establishment, besides being much more elaborately ornamented, was the center of the community life, possessing houses for his dependents, a special dance platform, a warriors' house, and a canoe house. In New Zealand a strange perversion of this tendency occurred. The great carved house, built to commemorate the birth of an heir to the principal chief, was conceived as the property of the chief; but he did not live in it, living instead in a small hut very little better, though perhaps slightly more decorated, than those of his fellow tribesmen. His store house was often especially decorated. Also, chiefs, because of their sacred character, had to perform certain parts of the work of house building, and were required to do all the work in constructing the house for the initiation of a priest's son. Ceremonial functions in this connection belonged to women of rank also. The Tahitian chief owned a large guest house, from which he often had to retire in order to accommodate his visitors. His establishment boasted several houses for different members of his family, was surrounded by a paved courtyard and a high fence, with the main house especially ornamented in a style similar to that of the guest house. Houses of chiefs were built by special levy. In Samoa the whole village united in building the platform for the new house of the chief. The reciprocal economic relations between a chief and a talking chief enabled him to pay the workers for his larger, better constructed house. Thus the connection between houses and rank is more intimate and universal than in the case of canoe building, but the psychology underlying the chief's possession of a better house had undergone a special development in each group.

The houses of all these cultures may be conceived as representing definite artistic attempts, only if perfection of workmanship and beauty of structure be included as well as actual decoration in the form of carving, paneling or sennit lashings. Colored sennit was used in Hawaii, Tahiti, the Marquesas, and recently in Samoa, — being the sole decoration in Hawaii, and used in streamers in Tahiti. Carving occurred only in New Zealand and the Marquesas; but here, although the likeness between the two groups when contrasted with other parts of the area is striking and significant, the two styles are distinctive and unmistakable. The Maori painting of carved work is unique[1], as are the patterned reed panels. The Samoan emphasis on perfection of structure is also a special development, being paralleled to some extent by the stress on durability in Hawaii, size in Tahiti, and actual decoration in the Marquesas and New Zealand.

---

[1] Only one painted house is reported in the Marquesas. Linton, R., Personal correspondence.

THE TATTOOING COMPLEX

DESCRIPTION.

Tattooing in Hawaii. — Tattooing was very slightly developed in Hawaii and the information is exceedingly scanty. Many of the early travellers do not even mention it, and those who do[1], comment upon the infrequency of the custom and the crudity of the design as compared with the tattooing in other groups.

The instruments used are not described in detail, but seem to have resembled those used throughout the area. Ellis[2] says the instrument was one-quarter of an inch wide, and set with small fish bones, and Meinicke[3] says there were three of these teeth. A round stick of wood was used as a mallet[4]. The pigment was made from the burnt aleurites, or candle-nut[3]. The design was faintly sketched in first; the instrument was dipped in the dye and then applied to the skin[5]. Legs, arms[6], trunk[7], (at least the front of the trunk), face, lips[8], and hands were sometimes all tattooed. The selection of the tongue for mourning tattooing is typically[8] Hawaiian[9]. It was sometimes the custom to tattoo alternate arms and legs[10].

There is no information available concerning the craftsmen, except a comment on their lack of skill[11]. Although the tattooing was performed very early in life[11], it is not known what relation it had to other aspects of puberty. The principal religious ramifications seem to have been the use of mourning tattoo marks, particularly on the tongue[12]. These marks were tattooed after a death; and when writing was introduced, the name of the dead king or relative was tattooed across the breast[13]. Alexander[14] says the women

---

[1] Ellis, *Journal,* p. 151; Bennet, Vol. I, p. 212; Remy, p. 15; Alexander, *Brief History,* p. 86; Meinicke, Vol. II, p. 293; Tyerman and Bennet, Vol. II, p. 24.
[2] *Journal,* pp. 136—137.
[3] Vol. II, p. 293.
[4] Roth, *Artificial Skin Markings of the Sandwich Islanders,* p. 200.
[5] Eveleth, p. 43.
[6] Krämer, *Hawaii, Ostmikronesien und Samoa,* p. 93; Roth, Op. Cit., p. 199, reproduction from Choris; Tyerman and Bennet, loc. cit.; Dixon, G., p. 98.
[7] Mager, p. 94.
[8] Ellis, op. cit., p. 134.
[9] Ibid., p. 136.
[10] Alexander, op. cit., p. 86.
[11] Tyerman and Bennet, Vol. II, p. 24.
[12] Ellis, op. cit., p. 136, and p. 151; Byron, p. 136; Alexander, op. cit., p. 86.
[13] Krämer, op. cit., p. 93.
[14] Op. cit., p. 56.

sometimes had the back of the hands tattooed, and Byron[1] says the women tattooed the tips of their tongues in mourning. No other sex differences are recorded.

One very definite connection with rank occurred, the outcast *Kauwa*, (slave) class were tattooed on the forehead[2]. King[3], speaks of property marks tattooed on the persons of the lower classes, and Eveleth[4], says tattoo marks served as a badge to distinguish the retainers of different chiefs. These statements may refer to the same phenomenon, the branding of the *Kauwa*. The chiefs were all tattooed on the tongue in the case of a death in the royal family[5].

The designs were of two types, free realistic representations and very simple geometric patterns. These latter resembled textile patterns and in one representation[6] the design seems to be a copy of a basketry effect, rather than a simple transfer of design. Small triangles arranged with their bases along vertical lines were used on the legs[7]. Intersecting straight lines seem to have been the commonest pattern[8]. A variety of realistic forms, trees, shrubs, birds, etc., were also used in fairly free combinations[9]. In Ellis's time goats were already being represented[10]. One picture in Krämer[7] shows a transverse arrangement of conventionalized birds on the breast, and Choris[6] recorded the tattooing of a tree adapted to the lines of the body. There seems to have been no zoning, nor is there any indication of fixed designs used for certain parts of the body.

Tattooing In The Marquesas. — The extent to which tattooing was developed in the Marquesas is paralleled only by the Maori tattooing. The technique follows the usual pattern, instruments like small adzes[11], made of fish bone[12], tortoise shell[11], and occasionally of human bone[13]. The handle of the instrument was of bamboo, as also was the mallet. The latter was twice as thick at one end, this thick part being about one-fifth of the length[14]. It was about three-quarters of an inch thick, and a foot to eighteen inches long. The blade was inserted in the handle of the instrument, a little distance from the end. The number of teeth varied from two to twelve, and

---

[1] Byron, p. 136.
[2] Malo, p. 101.
[3] Quoted by Roth, op. cit., p. 200.
[4] Eveleth, p. 43,
[5] Ellis, op. cit., p. 136, and p. 151; Byron, p. 136; Alexander, op. cit., p. 86.
[6] Roth, p. 199, reproduction from Choris.
[7] Kramer, op. cit., p. 93.
[8] Kotzebue, *New Voyages*, Vol. II, p. 174; Mager, p. 194.
[9] Bennet, p. 212; Portloch, p. 77; Cook, *Journal*, Vol. III, Chap. xii.
[10] Roth, op. cit., p. 199.
[11] Marchand, p. 99.
[12] Langsdorf, p. 118; Von den Steinen, p. 83.
[13] Handy, W. C., pp. 10—11: These were sometimes the bones of enemy sacrifices.
[14] Von den Steinen, p. 83, Fig. 37.

the instruments from 38 mm. long and 2 mm. wide to 78 mm. long and 14 mm. wide[1]. The blade was sometimes crescent shaped and sometimes straight[2]. The complete set was kept in a bamboo case[1], stoppered with a wad of tapa[3]. The soot from which the dye was made was derived from burned cocoa-nut shell[4] or burned aleurities[5]. The soot was collected on a small stone or in a cocoa-nut shell[6], and mixed with water or vegetable oil[7]. The design was first sketched on in charcoal, and the dye was rubbed on the comb by two fingers of the operator's right hand[8]. The blood was wiped away with a piece of tapa.

Men were tattooed on the top of the head, the face, including the eyebrows, the inside of the nostrils, the tongue, the palms and backs of hands, arms, legs and trunks. Women were tattooed to the base of the gums, the ear lobes, behind the ears, on the curve of the shoulders, on the hands, the legs, and from the buttocks down[9].

The procedure connected with tattooing was extremely elaborate,— including the construction of a special house for the tattooing of an eldest son *(opou)* by the *ka'ioi*, a more or less unorganized group of younger sons and daughters who were tattooed free while the *opou* was resting[10].

The craftsmen were itinerant artists, not organized in any guild[11]. Each artist ranked as a *tuhuna* and as such had charge of chanting genealogies and sacred songs, and Von den Steinen[12] believes he was also a healer. He was fed and housed by the family of the *opou*, and handsomely recompensed[11], — there being an initial agreement as to the amount[13]. The chief tattooer had four or five assistants who held the arms and legs of the patient, and sometimes filled in the lesser designs after he had outlined them[14]. The father was tabooed throughout the operation, and he, with the help of a virgin, mixed the pigment, but no strictly priestly functions are recorded[14].

The ceremonies of tattooing centered around the importance attributed to the *opou* or eldest son. A special house was built for him with a sleeping house and cook house attached. The younger sons and daughters, sometimes forty in all, raided the homes of the

---

[1] Von den Steinen, p. 83, abb. 37.
[2] Langsdorf, p. 118; Von den Steinen, p. 83.
[3] Handy, W. C., pp. 10—11.
[4] Porter, p. 124.
[5] Handy, W. C., p. 10; Von den Steinen, p. 84.
[6] Von den Steinen, p. 84, and Fig. 39.
[7] Berchon, p. 107.
[8] Handy, W. C., p. 11.
[9] Ibid., p. 14.
[10] Ibid., p. 7.
[11] Ibid., p. 9.
[12] Von den Steinen, p. 60.
[13] Langsdorf, p. 118.
[14] Handy, W. C., pp. 7—9.

relatives of the *opou* for food, building materials, and tapa with which to pay the tattooers. The morning on which the operation was to begin, drums were beaten to announce to the village the beginning of the taboo. The end of the operation was marked by a great feast at which the boys danced to show their new designs[1]. Boys were tattooed at puberty, girls at about twelve. A girl with an untattooed hand could not make *poipoi* or rub the bodies of the dead[2]. A tattooed hand could not eat from the same dish with an untattooed hand. No ceremonies were given for the girls' tattooing, but a chief occasionally gave a feast for a new design recently tattooed on his wife[3]. Tattoo marks were definitely associated with blood revenge[4], even women receiving a revenge tattoo mark, a fish hook design on the cheeks and neck. The patterns on older men were renewed several times, (Von den Steinen believes this was for protection in war[5].)

The whole emphasis was on the rank of the first born, as against the younger children.

The designs[6] were characterized by an extreme attention to zoning. Square and rectangular zones were filled in by intricate arrangements of small rectangular and curvilinear motifs. A few thinly disguised naturalistic designs occurred. The earlier tattooing[7] was characterized by large surfaces of very fine, almost uniform detail, and carefully observed zones. The zoning gave way to transverse tooth-edged sections, in the later development. The delicate minute patterns used to fill in the large spaces gave way to solid black surfaces, as the emphasis was more on the ability to bear pain; and chiefs who already possessed elaborate patterns would pay to have these obliterated by the solid black tattooing as witness to their fortitude.

Tattooing Among the Maori. — There were two types of tattooing in New Zealand,[8] — the elaborate curvilinear patterns of the northern Maori and the simple straight line tattooing of the southern Maori. Two kinds of instruments were used in the northern group, — one a small toothed adze, similar to that used throughout the Polynesian area, the other a sharp, single-pointed instrument, used in making the singular deep furrows, characteristic of the northern group[9]. The blade of the instrument was made of bone,[10] and attached to a wooden handle, which contained a fore-finger rest, and was

[1] Handy, W. C., p. 9; Von den Steinen, p. 85.
[2] Handy, W. C., p. 12.
[3] Ibid., p. 8.
[4] Langsdorf, p. 121; Von den Steinen, p. 64, Fig. 16.
[5] Ibid., p. 66.
[6] Figures and Plates in Handy and Von den Steinen.
[7] Von den Steinen, p. 144 et. seq.
[8] Skinner, H. D., *Culture Areas in New Zealand;* Polack, I, P. 45.
[9] Roth, *Maori Tatu and Moko;* Robley, p. 55.
[10] Roth, loc. cit.; Cruise, p. 136.

sometimes decorated. The single-pointed *moko* was like a chisel, about one millimeter broad and four millimeters long,[1] the blade being of whale bone.[2] One end of this instrument was shaped like a flat knife to wipe off the blood[3]. Pigment was made by burning several kinds of wood, or sometimes the vegetable caterpillar, in a small kiln.[4] The soot was collected on a frame of flat sticks and mixed with dog fat. It was either used in this form or fed to a dog, and the kneaded faeces used.[5] The pigment from the burnt *Kauri* gum was sometimes collected on a basket smeared with fat, and kept thus for generations.[4] The pattern was usually sketched on with a mixture of charcoal and water,[6] or with a sharp point.[7] The instrument was either dipped in the pigment,[8] or the operator held a little of the pigment between the thumb and fore-finger, and drew the chisel through it.[9] The blood was wiped away with a piece of flax,[10] a wooden spatula,[11] or the end of the instrument.[4]

Men were tattooed on the face, the upper part of the trunk, and on the thigh to the knee. Occasionally the tip of the tongue was tattooed[12]. Women were tattooed on the lips, and sometimes between breast and navel, on the lower abdomen, on the thigh[13], and on the hands and arms[14]; but more usually they had only a sparse design on the lips and chin[15].

The professional tattooers were well paid itinerant individuals[16]. Slaves who knew the art were immediately freed.

The religious aspect was particularly emphasized by the stringent taboos. During the process the whole village was taboo[17], and the patients were not allowed to feed themselves with their own hands[18]. At the conclusion of the operation, three ovens were lighted, — one for the artificers, one for the gods, one for the newly tattooed and the rest of the people; the priest, by a ceremony of cooking food which was then ceremonially eaten, freed the people from the taboo[19]. A human victim, to obtain whom a war party was dispatched, was

---

[1] Roth, *Maori Tatu and Moko;* Robley, p. 55.
[2] Tregear, p. 258.
[3] Ibid., p. 259.
[4] Roth, op. cit., p. 41.
[5] Robley, p. 157.
[6] Tregear, pp. 258—259.
[7] Polack, I, p. 46.
[8] Roth, p. 41—42.
[9] Best, *The Maori*, Vol. II, p. 554; *The New Zealanders*, p. 137.
[10] The *New Zealanders*, p. 137.
[11] D'Urville, Vol. II, p. 448.
[12] Best, *The Maori*, II, p. 557.
[13] Tregear, p. 265.
[14] Roth, p. 33.
[15] Robley, pp. 33—38.
[16] Polack, II, p. 58; Tregear, p. 258.
[17] *The New Zealanders*, p. 138.
[18] Robley, p. 59; Tregear, p. 265.
[19] Roth, pp. 42—44.

sacrificed[1] when a chief's daughter had her lips tattooed. Contrary to the usual Polynesian practice, tattooing was done, not at puberty, but after full growth was attained[2]. Women were always tattooed on the lips before marriage[3]. Definite tattoo marks were not used as badges of mourning, but the ceremonial cuts women made on their bodies'were filled in with pigment[4], and this dyeing of scarification marks constitutes a real variation in technique[5]. Heads of dead relatives were sometimes tattooed[6].

Tattooing was more definitely associated with war than with rank. Slaves taken in childhood[7] were not tattooed. But many chiefs were not tattooed at all[8], and priests are said to have had only a small blotch over one eye[9]. New tattoo marks were sometimes assumed by all the warriors of the tribe before going to war[10].

The designs used by the southern tribes[11] were simple series of parallel lines, arranged in groups of three or four, alternately vertical and horizontal. The only curvilinear element was an S-like figure in the middle of the forehead[12]. The designs[13] used by the northern tribes were all curvilinear, and elaborately stylized in respect to the sex of the wearer, and the part of the body to be decorated. Great emphasis was placed on the conformance of the design to the shape of the chin, the cheek, etc. The thigh pattern and the scroll used on each buttock were unvariable; but the smaller units used on the face permitted great individuality of arrangement, although all of these were based on a few curvilinear motifs. Roth[14] distinguished seven motifs: lines of dots or strokes, mat or plait work, ladder, chevron, circinate scroll, anchor, and trilateral scroll.

Tattooing in Tahiti[15]. — The tools used in Tahitian tattooing were the typical toothed adzes of varying sizes, and also a sharp single pointed tool resembling the Maori *moko* tool[16]. The handles of the

---

[1] Best, *Maori Religion and Mythology*, Sec. I, p. 145.
[2] Robley, (p. 38) thinks this is because further growth would distort lines.
[3] Tregear, p. 265.
[4] Roth, p. 34; Robley, p. 45.
[5] Best, *The Maori*, Vol. II, p. 546.
[6] Roth, p. 44.
[7] Dieffenbach, Vol. II, p. 34.
[8] Roth, p. 49. (Quotes Yate); Polack, I, p. 47.
[9] Savage, p. 48.
[10] Earle, p. 13; Savage, p. 47.
[11] Best, *The Maori*, II, p. 549, 552; Tregear, p. 263; Cowan, p. 193; Beattie, p. 221; Roth, p. 134.
[12] White, Vol. I, Frontispiece.
[13] Reproductions in Robley and Roth.
[14] Roth, p. 34.
[15] Our information on tattooing in the Society Islands is also very sparse. It received no such impetus as did the Maori tattooing from the traffic in heads, and was early discouraged by the missionaries, although there seems to have been a temporary and poorly recorded efflorescense just before the practice began to die out. This latter fact is suggested by a comparison of accounts of the Forsters and of Ellis 40 years later.
[16] Roth, *Tatu in the Society Islands*, pp. 283—94.

tools were of wood, and sometimes possessed a curved four-finger rest. The teeth ranged in number from three to twenty; the instruments were about five inches long, and one-half an inch wide[1]. The blade and handle were bound together with bark string. The mallet was a paddle shaped stick, heavier than the instrument itself, having a gradually tapering handle[2]. The blade was made of shell or the bones of birds or fishes[3]. The dye was made from the kernel of the aleurites nut, baked, reduced to charcoal, pulverized, and mixed with cocoa-nut oil[3]. The design was first traced on with charcoal[4], the operator sometimes imprinting guide circles by bending a leaf stem into a circle, dipping it into the dye and applying it to the stick[5]. The instrument was dipped in the dye, and the perforation accomplished by a sharp rap with the mallet[6].

Women were tattooed on the buttocks[7], on the feet and ankles, and the hands and wrists[8]. The women were tattooed more sparingly than the men[8], but what areas of the men's bodies were tattooed is not recorded. They were certainly tattooed on the legs[4], the trunk, the thighs, and the face[9].

There were special tattooing experts who were employed[10], and well remunerated in cloth and food[7]. Bennett[11] speaks of the profession being followed particularly by hunchbacks. These operations seem to have been of a definitely religious character[7], and the work was prefaced by offerings to the two divine patrons of tattooing[12]. The instruments used in tattooing chiefs or eldest sons were destroyed at the *marai* as soon as the work was completed[13]. The tattooing of boys was begun at the age of eight to ten[14], while the arches on the girls' buttocks were considered to be marks of attained puberty[15]. Ellis's[8] mention of immoral practices accompanying tattooing suggests a festival. Tattoo marks were occasionally adopted as badges of mourning, but this was not a common custom[14]. A small spot was tattooed on the inside of a child's arm as a sign that the child was free from taboo and might touch its parents' food[16].

---

[1] Roth, *Tatu in the Society Islands*, p. 286. MS. Cook Expedition.
[2] Ibid., pp. 283—94.
[3] Ellis, *Researches*, p. 206; Meinicke, II, p. 173.
[4] Ellis, I, p. 207.
[5] Bennet, p. 120.
[6] Banks, p. 25.
[7] Forster, G., p. 557.
[8] Ellis, I, p. 208.
[9] Roth, op. cit., Plates.
[10] Ellis, I, p. 206; Wilson, p. 339.
[11] Page 117.
[12] Ellis, I, p. 206.
[13] Wilson, p. 342.
[14] Ellis, I, p. 205.
[15] Forster, G., p. 555; Cook, *Journal* (Wharton Edition), p. 73.
[16] Wilson, p. 339.

Tattooing was practiced by all classes[1]. Special patterns were used to distinguish the seven orders of the Areois Society[2].

With the exception of puberty marks for girls, the arm marks, and the devices used among the Areois, there was little conventionalization of the designs with particular significance[3]. Both geometric figures, such as stars, circles, and lozenges, were used, as were also a large number of realistic designs which sometimes depicted whole scenes. The hospitality shown to representations of foreign objects, such as muskets, swords, etc., suggests a flexible arrangement of motifs and lack of conventionalization. The few designs[4] which are extant make only positive statements possible. The herring-bone and tooth lines were used, and triangles in a variety of combination. One drawing[5] shows the use of rather heavy design units, the drawing of Gerstaecker[6] shows a realistic fish combined with a semi-geometric design, containing hour-glass patterns.

Tattooing In Samoa. — The Samoan tattooing instruments were of the universal small adze type, about six inches long, with a serrated edge like a comb[7]. The blades were made of human bone, or of tortoise shell[8]; the handles were of reed[7], or wood[8]. The mallet was a long stick, widened at one end[9]. A complete set consisted of a number of instruments of different sizes; they were kept in a special wooden case, together with the cocoa-nut shell which held the pigment[10].

The men were usually tattooed from calf to navel[11], and sometimes on the upper parts of the body[12] as well. Women were tattooed more lightly on hands, arms, and legs, and on the area just above the groin. The face was never tattooed except in the case of the nose which was a definite form of punishment[13] in Western Samoa.

The boys were tattooed between the ages of twelve and fifteen. A number of boys of the same age were tattooed with the chief's son, ceremoniously "sharing his pain", and the expenses of their tattooing were paid by the chief's family[14]. The families of these youths were also recompensed by the present of a mat. Four or five youths were usually tattooed together[15], and an equal number of operators

---

[1] Ellis, I, p. 205.
[2] Ibid., p. 189.
[3] Ellis, II, pp. 206—208.
[4] Roth, op. cit., Plates XXIII and XXIV.
[5] Ibid., Plate XXIII.
[6] Von den Steinen, p. 149, Fig. 96.
[7] Pritchard, p. 145.
[8] Marquardt, p. 9.
[9] Krämer, *Die Samoa Inseln*, Vol. II, p. 75.
[10] Ibid., p. 74; Marquardt, p. 9.
[11] Stair, p. 160.
[12] Marquardt, Figures.
[13] Stair, p. 101.
[14] Ibid., p. 158.
[15] Turner, p. 89.

might be summoned. The chief operators brought their instruments
and they seemed to have had a train of assistants[1]. The operators
brought their families with them, and a special house was erected in
the center of the village[2]. This house was taboo to the boy's female
relatives, whom he called *"tuafafine"*. No food could be taken into
it. A great feast opened the proceedings, which included a sham
fight and the initial payment to the artists[3]. The operation sometimes took as long as three months, and the whole period was regarded as one of festivity. There were many visitors in the village
and sham fights, wrestling, boxing, and dancing beguiled the time[4].
The other payments were made when the operation was half
completed, and when only the tattooing of the navel remained[5].
Marquardt[6] considers the tattooer to have been a priest, accusing
the priests of having usurped a profitable secular profession; but
Turner[7], Stair[8], and Pritchard[9], all speak of the tattooers as an
organized group of craftsmen, resembling the house builders and
canoe builders. In eastern Samoa they were not organized, but
worked as individual artists. However, the taboo-lifting ceremony[9]
which concluded the operations seems to have had supernatural
reference and in this the tattooers officiated.

The evening before this ceremony, operators, attendants, and
newly tattooed youths repaired to the *malae* with lighted torches.
The torches were extinguished and a water bottle (a gourd) was
dashed to pieces in front of the young chief. The next day the
whole group were sprinkled with water from a cocoa-nut shell by
one of the operators. The tattooing of women was a minor matter,
unmarked by festival or rite[10]. Girls were debarred from no activity
because not yet tattooed, but untattooed boys were segregated in
the *aumaga*, the organization of untitled men, and forbidden to
make kava or *tafolo*.

Rank was very definitely and commercially bound up with
tattooing, — the youths of lesser importance being tattooed with
the chief's sons, although Stair says[11] this form of tattooing is looked
down upon. Youths were tattooed in order of rank[12]. The bottle was
broken only in front of a chief. When the son of a very important
chief was tattooed, the operation was made the occasion of a gathering of people from all over the district[11].

---

[1] Stair, p. 159; Pritchard, p. 143.
[2] Marquardt, p. 10; Stair, p. 160.
[3] Stair, loc. cit.
[4] Ibid., p. 136; Marquardt, p. 11.
[5] Pritchard, p. 144.
[6] Page 17.
[7] Page 89.
[8] Page 164.
[9] Stair, pp. 163—164.
[10] Turner, p. 91.
[11] Page 158.
[12] Pritchard, p. 143.

Mrs. Handy[1] obtained accounts in Western Samoa of definite patterns associated with and restricted to the two ranks of chiefs and talking chiefs. In Eastern Samoa no particular design was so restricted but if several boys of different ranks were tattooed together, the most elaborate design, the largest number of bands and triangles, must be put on the boy of highest lineage, the sons of the chiefs outranking the sons of talking chiefs. This is consistent with the Eastern Samoan arrangement by which a high chief had more terraces to his house than a talking chief, but no set number was necessary. Analogous to the fact that the *Tui Tonga* was too sacred to be tattooed by one of his subjects is the usage relating to the *Tui Manu'a*, the sacred high chief of the Manu'a Archipelago. If so be it he had been tattooed before he was consecrated, well and good; but once consecrated, no one could draw his blood.

The elements of the design were the same for both sexes, but the arrangement was radically different[2]. In the case of the women, the designs were scattered sparsely, with careful regard for symmetry, over the parts of the body decorated, while in men's tattooing, these elements occurred only in the occasional narrow spaces left in an otherwise completely tattooed surface. The commonest motives were the flying foxes which occur also in various reduced forms, four and eight pointed stars, herring-bone series, and arrangements of dots. A special series of dots on the inner arm may have been either individual identification marks[3], or district marks[4]. The navel was the last part tattooed[5], and invariably, in a design known as the bat's wing[6].

ANALYSIS OF TATTOOING.

The core of the tattooing complex was a uniformity of technique, in which a dye made of soot mixed with oil or water was pricked into the skin in decorative designs, by a toothed adze-like instrument. Both men and women were tattooed throughout the area, and there was definite specialization of the craftsmen.

The variations in the technique were negligible, except in the case of the single-pointed, deeper-cutting *moko* tool of the northern Maori[7], and the treatment of scarification marks among the Maori. The size of the blade and the length of the mallet varied from group to group, and preference was sometimes for bone and sometimes for

---

[1] Handy, W. C., *Samoan Tattooing*, p. 21.
[2] Marquardt, Figures.
[3] Ibid., p. 24.
[4] Pritchard, p. 145. Some such form of identification is made plausible by the fact that relatives claimed the bodies of the slain, although the bodies of the slain were decapitated. Brown, G., p. 170.
[5] Pritchard, p. 140.
[6] Brown, G., p. 100.
[7] The same tool occurred in Tahiti; see p. 76.

shell, etc., but the essential features were constant. In all parts of the area the design was sometimes, though not always, sketched on first; in Tahiti the special device of a circular bamboo fiber was used. The blood was wiped away with tapa or flax, and in New Zealand the other end of the tool was sometimes shaped for this purpose. The parts of the body decorated varied considerably, — the Samoans never tattooing on the face for decorative purposes. The thigh design was most universal and received the most conventionalized treatment. The women in all cases were less decorated than the men, except possibly in Southern New Zealand. The craftsman assumed ceremonial functions in Samoa and possibly in the Marquesas. He was definitely professional throughout the area, and handsomely paid. His prestige was greatest in Samoa and New Zealand, and probably least in Hawaii.

The connection with puberty was definite in Tahiti and the Marquesas, lacking in the case of boys in New Zealand, and problematical in Hawaii. Festivals accompanied tattooing in Samoa, and probably in Tahiti. Human sacrifices are reported for New Zealand alone. Tattooing was connected with mourning in New Zealand and the Marquesas, where the mourning cuts were filled in with pigment, and in Tahiti and Hawaii where memorial patterns were used. The mourning aspect was the chief emphasis in Hawaii. Tattoo marks were memorials of revenge obligations in the Marquesas, and used as community-enforced punishment in Samoa. Strict taboos surrounded the tattooing in New Zealand and the Marquesas, but these taboos varied in content; men could not bathe in the Marquesas; in New Zealand they could not feed themselves with their own hands while undergoing the operation. The taboo was lifted by food ceremonies in New Zealand, bathing in the Marquesas, and sprinkling in Samoa. The design varied from group to group, from the use of the circle and geometrical forms in close association with a very free application of realistic designs in Tahiti, to the textile patterns and sparse rectilinear designs in Hawaii, the heavy solid tattooing, with occasional more lightly decorated spacing on Samoan men, and the scanty application of the filling-in designs to the Samoan women, to the elaborate and artistic developments of the Maori and the Marquesans; in the first place the adaptation with scroll to every part of the body decorated, in the second a multiplicity of elements arranged in definite zones.

CONCLUSIONS

An attempt has been made to investigate the stability of the different elements involved in the complex of activities centering about canoe building, house building, and tattooing in five insular cultures of Polynesia. In the case of canoe building, variations in technique and variations in mechanical principles were found to be very rare. The relative prestige and importance of priest and crafts-man varied tremendously from Hawaii, where the priest performed the skilled parts of the work and the builders were held in low esteem, to Samoa, where the priest had no function at all, and the builders were enormously powerful. But the importance and prestige of these two professions were found not to vary inversely because the ceremonial prerogatives and duties of rank in New Zealand distorted such a negative correlation, — leaving some parts of the work *neither* to priest nor craftsman, but to the chief. The taboos varied in strength from a taboo which covered the whole course of the operation and all who participated in it in the Marquesas, to a mere formal technique for excluding intruders in Samoa. The content of the taboos, with the emphasis on contamination from women or food, infringement by intrusion or noise as the case might be, was seen to be even more variable. The religious ceremonies,— when they occurred, — followed to some extent a logical pattern imposed by the stages in the construction of a canoe, but this same series or steps was marked by formal payment of the workers in Samoa, instead of offerings to the gods as in Tahiti or sacred chants as in the other groups. The extent to which the canoe entered into the re-ligious complex of each group also showed difference, — the sacred canoes definitely dedicated to a god's service being peculiar to Tahiti, the sacredness of the canoe *per se*, as demonstrated by the aura of canoes being greatest in the Marquesas, and the canoe having a purely secular character in Samoa. The connection with rank seems to have been almost completely fortuitous.

In house building, the basic structure and the important technical principles of ridge pole, sliding-door[1], the use of lashings and joints, bonnetting of roof with the help of a supplementary ridge pole, showed very slight deviations. The most definite individualization occurred in the shape and appearance of the house, and this must be attributed not only to the instability of the shape, but also to its dependence upon the materials used. The substitution of grass for sugar-cane leaves or of reeds for heavy slabs of wood produces a

---

[1] The door did not occur in Samoa.

change in appearance disproportionate to the changes which have really occurred. When this variation in material is combined with such structural variation as the round ground plan in Samoa, the steep rear roof in the Marquesas, or the hip-roof of Hawaii, a unique form of house is found in each group. If the form of the house is taken to be closely allied with the decoration of the house, (as the shape of the stern and bow pieces might be considered to be in the case of canoe building), these two aspects, taken together may be said to be most individually developed. The style of decoration is fundamentally different in each of the four groups where decoration occurs, as is also the particular emphasis on beauty of structure in Samoa. The priest performed some ceremonies in the Marquesas, New Zealand, and Hawaii, but these differed considerably. The craftsman was simply a man more skillful than his neighbor, but not strictly a professional in Hawaii, while in other groups he enjoyed great prestige. The division of houses according to function (perhaps originally associated coherently with the various taboo operations) varied from household specialization in Hawaii to village specialization in New Zealand, and the degree to which these houses were sacred, and the uses to which they were put had undergone great reinterpretation. The taboos attach themselves indiscriminately to various parts of the house. The connection with rank was partly dictated by the wealth and prestige incident to rank, but this did not prevent the Maori chief from residing in a mean hut, while nominally owning the great carved house. The relationship between the chief's establishment and the community varied from its great importance in the Marquesas, to very little importance in Hawaii.

In tattooing the technique was even more constant than in either of the preceding complexes, but this is explicable in terms of the relative simplicity of the process as compared with canoe building, for example. The style of decoration was unique and specially developed in each area; the closest associations seem to be between Hawaii and Southern New Zealand, but here the simplicity of the design may overweigh the apparent resemblance. The parts of the body decorated also varied, but the tendency to tattoo men more completely and elaborately than women was a more constant feature. The status of the craftsman was less definite, but he seems to have enjoyed greatest individual renown among the Maori, general ceremonial functions in the Marquesas, and specific ceremonial unctions in Samoa. The priest played an important part only in New Zealand. The relation of tattooing to puberty, in the case of boys, to puberty and marriage in the case of girls, follows no definite lines. The peculiar development of tattooing in New Zealand necessitated tattooing of adults, as did its use for mourning in Hawaii. The content of the taboos and rites was different in each group.

6*

Thus, in these three complexes all having a definite technique, a style of art, religio-ceremonial relationships, craft specialization, and some relation to rank, there is found to be least variation in technique and especially in function, and most in form and style of decoration. The other elements, and this includes decorative art also in the case of house-building, vary from maximum development in one area, as ceremonialism in Hawaii, decorative art in the Marquesas and New Zealand, prestige of craftsmen in Samoa, duties through rank in New Zealand, and exemption from work in Hawaii, to a very weak development in other island groups as decorative art in Tahiti, or connection between rank and canoe building in the Marquesas, to almost nonexistence in other groups, as decoration in Samoa and prestige of craftsmen in Hawaii. That some of these elements might have disappeared entirely in a few hundred years is suggested by the weakening of the religious complex in Samoa, and the little emphasis upon decorative tattooing in Hawaii. In any case, the religio-ceremonial elements, the status of priests and craftsmen, and the connection with social class seems to be fortuitous, immensely variable in detail, and particularly subject to reinterpretation in terms of the prevailing pattern of each group.

General application of these conclusions is limited by the fact that they are based upon the examination of only three aspects of one culture, but, while the positive conclusions, i. e., that technique, particularly functional variation, is most stable and form as expressed by shape, size, etc., and decorative elements are most variable, cannot be claimed as necessarily true for other areas, the negative conclusions can be so generalized. This study indicates that if in this one area, taboos, rituals, religious significances, prerogatives of rank, and questions of professional status are found to be so variable and sensitive to reinterpretation, then evidence of this type is manifestly unreliable data on whi h to base historical reconstructions. Elements whi h do vary as mu h as these, whi h yield so swiftly to the cultural emphasis within one small area, are not valid data for the study, for instance, of possible culture contact between Oceania and the Americas, or Africa and Melanesia.

BIBLIOGRAPHY

The type of material available for Polynesia is in peculiar need of biblio-graphical annotation, as many of the titles are unspecific and misleading. Accordingly, when any work listed in this bibliography has been used as an authority on any group, to which its title makes no reference, an abbreviation of the name of this group will be placed in parenthesis after the name of the work. These abbreviations are: Hawaii (H), the Marquesas (M), the Maori of New Zealand (NZ), Tahiti and the other Society Islands (T), and Samoa (S).

The following list contains works specifically referred to in the text, or those which have been extensively utilized in obtaining the background for this study. It is by no means a complete bibliography of the subject. For the assistance of other research workers in this field, a list of available special bibliographies is appended.

A. M. N. H. followed by a number refers to specimens in the American Museum of Natural History, New York.

ABBREVIATIONS OF PERIODICALS

Australian Association for the Advancement of Science — A. A. A. S.
Journal of the Polynesian Society — J. P. S.
Journal of the Royal Anthropological Institute of Great Britain and Ireland — J. R. A. I.
Internationales Archive für Ethnographie — I. A. f. E.
Transactions of the New Zealand Institute — T. N. Z. I.

Alexander, A. B.: "Notes on the Boats, Apparatus and Fishing Methods Employed by the Natives of the South Sea Islands and Results of Fishing Trials by the Albatross". *U. S. Commission of Fish and Fisheries, Commissioner's Report*, 1901, pp. 741—829.
Alexander, W. D.: *A Brief History of the Hawaiian People*, 1891.
Anderson, J. C.: *Maori Life in Ao-tea*, Wellington, 1907.
Angas, G. F.: *Savage Life and Scenes in Australia and New Zealand*, 2nd ed., London, 1847.
Banks, J.: *Journal of the Right Hon. Sir Joseph Banks, Bart. K. B. P. R. S.* Edited by Sir Joseph D. Hooker, London, 1896.
Barstow, A. C.: *The Maori Canoe*, T. N. Z. I., Vol. II, 1868, p. 71.
Beattie, H.: *Traditions and Legends Collected from the Natives of Murihiku (Southland, N. Z.)*, Part VIII, J. P. S., Vol. XXVII, pp. 137—163.
   Ibid., Part XI, J. P. S., Vol. XXVIII, pp. 212—231.
Bennett, F. D.: *Narrative of a Whaling Voyage Around the Globe From the Years 1830 to 1836*, London, 1840.
Berchon, A.: *Le Tatouage aux Iles Marquise*, Bull. Soc. d'Anthropologie de Paris, Vol. I, pp. 99—117.
Best, Eldson: *The Maori*, Memoirs of the Pol. Soc. Vol. II, 1924.
— *The Maori Canoe*, Bul. Dominion Museum, No. 7, 1926.
— *Maori Religion and Mythology*, Sect. I, Bul. Dominion Museum, No. 10, 1924.
— *Maori Voyagers and their Vessels: How the Maori Explored the Pacific Ocean and Laid Down the Sea Roads for All Time*, T. N. Z. I., Vol. 48, p. 447.
— *The Peopling of New Zealand*, Man, 1914, No. 37.
Bingham, C.: *A History of Hawaii*.

Bishop, S.: *Reminiscences of Serano Bishop;* Edited by L. Thurston, Honolulu, 1911.

Bougainville, Louis de: *Voyage Around the World Performed by Order H. M. in the Years 1756, 7, 8, 9.*, translated from the French by J. R. Forster, London, 1772.

Brigham, W. T.: *Housebuilding of the Old Hawaiians With a Description of the Articles Used in Housebuilding,* Mem. B. P. Bishop Museum, Vol. II.

Brown, George: *Melanesians and Polynesians,* New York, 1910. (S):

Brown, J. M.: *Maori and Polynesian,* London, 1907.

Brown, William: *New Zealand and its Aborigines,* London, 1845.

Buller, J.: *Forty Years in New Zealand,* 1878.

Byron: *Voyages of H. M. Ship Blond to the Sandwich Islands in the Years 1824—1825.* (H)

Cheever, H. T.: *The Island World of the Pacific,* 1851. (H)

Christian, F. W.: *The Eastern Pacific Islands, Tahiti, and the Marquesas,* London, 1910.

Churchill, W.: *Club Types of Nuclear Polynesia,* Carnegie Institution Pub. 255.

— *The Polynesian Wanderings,* Washington, D. C., 1911.

— *Sissano movements of Migration within and through Melanesia,* Carnegie Institute, 1916.

Churchward, W. B.: *My Consulate in Samoa,* London, 1887.

Coan, T.: *Life in Hawaii,* 1882. (M)

Cobb, J. N.: *Commercial Fisheries of the Hawaiian Islands,* U. S. Fish Commission, Commissioner's Report, 1901, pp. 381—499.

Colenso, W.: *On the Maori Races of New Zealand,* T. N. Z. I., Vol. I, pp. 340—422, 1867.

— *Notes and Reminiscences of Early Crossings of the Romant, etc.,* T. N. Z. I., Vol. 27, p. 400, 1894.

Cook, James: *Voyages Toward the South Pole and Round the World,* London, W. Strahan and T. Cadell, 1777.

— *The Voyages of Captain James Cook in Two Volumes,* London, Wm. Smith, 1842.

Corney, P.: *Voyages in the North Pacific,* 1896. (H)

Cowan, James: *The Maoris of New Zealand,* 1909.

Crawfurd, I. C.: *Recollections of Travels in New Zealand and Australia,* 1880.

Cruise, R.A.: *Journal of a Ten Months Residence in New Zealand,* London, 1823.

Demandt, E.: *Die Fischerei der Samoaner,* Mitteilungen aus dem Museum für Völkerkunde in Hamburg, III, 1913.

Dibble, Sheldon: *A History of the Sandwich Islands,* 1909.

Dieffenbach, E.: *Travels in New Zealand,* London, 1843.

Dixon, George A.: *A Voyage Round the World, but More Particularly to the Northwest Coast of America . . . in the "King George" and the "Queen Charlotte",* 2nd ed., London, 1789. (H)

Dixon, R. B.: "A New Theory of the Polynesian Race", Proceedings Am. Philos. Soc., Vol. IX, No. 4, 1920, p. 261.

— *Oceanic Mythology* (see Gray, L. H., *The Mythology of All Races,* Vol. IX).

D'Urville, J. Dumont: *Voyage de l'Astrolabe. . . Pendant les annees 1826-1829 sous le commandement de M. J. Dumant D'Urville,* Paris, 1833—1834. (T) (NZ)

Earle, A.: *Narrative of a Nine Months Residence in 1827, in New Zealands,* 1909.

Edge-Partington, J.: *An Album of Weapons, Tools, Ornaments, etc.,* privately printed.

Ella, S.: "Samoa", A. A. A. S., Vol. VI, 1892, p. 622.

Ellis, W.: *Journal of William Ellis: A Narrative of A Tour Through the Sandwich Islands, in 1823,* Honolulu, 1917.

Ellis, W.: *Polynesian Researches,* in two volumes, London, 1829 (T)

Emerson, N. B.: "The Long Voyages of the Ancient Hawaiians," Haw. Hist. Soc. Papers, 1893.

Emory, K.: *The Island of Lanai*, B. P. B. Mus., Bull. XII, 1924.
Erskine, J. E.: *Journal of a Cruise Among the Islands of the Western Pacific*, London, 1853, (S).
Eveleth, E.: *Letters* (H).
Fornander, A.: *An Account of the Polynesian Race*, 1878.
Fornander Collection of Hawaiian Antiquities and Folklore, 3rd series, edited by Thomas G. Thrum, Mem. B. P. Bishop Museum, Vol. VI, 1920.
Foster, G.: *A Voyage Round the World in His Britannic Majesty's Ship Resolution, commanded by Captain James Cook, during the Years 1772, 3, 4, 5*, London, 1777. (H) (T).
Foster, John R.: *Observations Made During a Voyage Round the World*, London, 1768, (T) (M).
Fox, H. L.: "On Early Modes of Navigation", J. R. A. I., IV, 1875, pp. 399—430.
Frazer, J. G.: *The Belief in Immortality and the Worship of the Dead*, Vol. II, *The Belief Among the Polynesians*, New York, 1922.
Garnier, J.: *Océanie: Les Iles des Paque, Loyalty et Tahiti*, 1871.
Gill, W. W.: *Jottings from the Pacific*, London, 1885. (Cook group).
— *Life in the Southern Isles*, London, 1876.
— *Myths and Songs from the Southern Pacific*, London, 1876.
Graebner, F.: *Die Methode der Ethnologie*, Heidelberg, 1911.
Greiner, R. H.: *Polynesian Decorative Design*, B. P. Bishop Museum, Bul. No. 7, 1923.
Haddon, A. C.: "The Outrigger Canoes of Torres Straits and N. Queensland", (In *Essays and Studies Presented to William Ridgeway*), 1923.
— "The Outriggers of Indonesian Canoes", J. R. A. I., Vol. 50, pp. 69—134.
Hale, H.: *Ethnology and Philology of the U. S. Exploring Expedition*, U. S. Explo. Exped., Vol. IV, 1846.
Hamilton, A.: *The Art Workmanship of the Maori Race in New Zealand*, Wellington, 1896.
Handy, E. C. S.: *The Native Culture in the Marquesas*, B. P. Bishop Museum, Bull. No. 9, 1923.
— "The Oracle House in Polynesia", J. P. S. Vol. 35, p. 47.
— *Samoan House Building, Cooking and Tattooing*, B. P. Bishop Museum Bull. 15, 1924.
Handy, W. C.: *Tattooing in the Marquesas*, B.P. Bishop Museum, Bull. No. 1, 1923.
Hood, T. H.: *Notes of a Cruise in H. M. Ship Fawn in the W. Pacific . . . in the Year 1862*, Edinburgh, 1863, (S).
Hornell, J.: "*The Outrigger Canoes of Indonesia*", Madras Fisheries Bulletin, Vol. XII, pp. 43—114, 1920.
Hugenin, P.: *Raiatea la Sacree*, 1901. (T).
Jarves, J. J.: *History of the Hawaiian Islands*, Honolulu, 1847.
Kotzebue, O. von: *Voyage of Discovery into the South Seas and Beerings Straits . . . Undertaken in the Years 1815 etc.*, London, 1821 (T).
Krämer, A.: *Die Samoa-Inseln*, Stuttgart, 1902.
— *Hawaii, Ostmikronesien und Samoa*, Stuttgart, 1906.
Krustenstern, A. J. von: *Voyage around the World in the Years 1803-4-5-6:*, translated from the German by Richard Belgrave Hoppner, Vol. I, London, 1813, (M).
Langsdorf, G. H. von: *Voyages and Travels in Various Parts of the World during the Years 1803—1807*, London, 1813. (M).
Laurence, N. L.: *Old Time Hawaiians and their Work*, New York, 1912.
Linton, R.: *The Material Culture of the Marquesas Islands*, Memoir B. P. Bishop Mus., Vol. VIII, No. 5, 1923.
New Zealanders, The. (The Library of Entertaining Knowledge, published under the Supervision of the Society for the Diffusion of Useful Knowledge), London, 1830.
Mager, H.: *Le Monde Polynesian*, Paris, 1902. (H).

Malo, David: *Hawaiian Antiquities:* translated by Dr. N. B. Emerson, Honolulu, 1903.
Marchand, E.: *Voyage autour du Monde pendant les annees 1790, 1791, et 1792.* Paris, An. VI—VIII (M).
Marcuse, A.: *Die Hawaiischen Inseln*, 1894.
Mariner, W.: *An Account of the Natives of the Tonga Islands in the South Pacific Ocean: Compiled and Arranged from Extensive Communications of Mr. Mariner by John Martin, M. D.*, Edinburgh, 1822.
Marquardt, C.: *Die Tätowierung beider Geschlechter in Samoa*, Berlin 1899.
Marshall, W. B.: *Two Visits to New Zealand in H. M. S. "Alligator".* 1834.
Meares, J.: *Voyages made in the years 1788 and 1789 from China to N. W. Coast of America*, etc., London, 1791. (H).
Meinicke, C. E.: *Die Inseln des Stillen Oceans*, Leipzig, 1888.
Mellville, H.: *Marquesas Islands*, 1846.
Moerenhout, J. A.: *Voyages aux Iles du Grand Ocean*, Paris, 1837. (T)
Murray, A. W.: *Forty Years Missionary Work in Polynesia and New Guinea, 1835—1875*, London, 1876. (S).
Parkinson, S.: *A Journal of a Voyage to the South Seas in H. M. S. "The Endeavor"*, London, 1773.
Perry, W. J.: *The Children of the Sun*, London, 1923.
Polack, J. S.: *Manners and Customs of the New Zealanders*, London, 1840.
Porter, D.: *Journal of a Cruise Made to the Pacific Ocean by Capt. David Porter ... in the years 1812, 13, and 14*, Philadelphia, 1815. (M)
Portlock, N.: *A Voyage around the World and more particularly to the North West Coast of America ... in the "King George" and "Queen Charlotte"*, 1786. (H)
Pritchard, W. T.: *Polynesian Reminiscences*, London, 1866. (S)
Rivers, W. H. R.: *The History of Melanesian Society*, Cambridge, 1914.
Robley, H. G.: *Moko or Maori Tattooing*, London, 1896.
Rosenberg, H. von: "Mentawei", I. A. f. E., Vol. I., 1888, pp. 218—219.
Roth, H. L.: "Artificial Skin Marking in the Sandwich-Islands", I. A. f. E., Vol. 13, pp. 198—201.
— "Maori Tatu and Moko", J. R. A. I. New Series, Vol. IV., p. 24.
— "Tatu in the Society Islands", J. R. A. I. Vol. 35, 1905, pp. 283—94.
— "Tonga Islanders' Skin Marking", Man, 1906, No. 4.
Routledge, Mrs. Scoresby: *The Mystery of Easter Island*, London, 1919.
Savage, J.: *Some Account of New Zealand, particularly the Bay of Islands, with a Description of their Religion and Government*, etc., 1807.
Shortland, E.: *Traditions and Superstitions of the New Zealanders*, London, 1856.
Skinner, H. D.: "*Culture Areas in New Zealand*", J. P. S.Vol. XXX, pp. 77—78.
— *The Morioris of Chatham Island*, Mem. B. P. Bishop Museum, Vol. IX, No. 1.
— "*Monck's Cave*", Canterbury Museum Records, II, p. 4, pp. 151—162, 1924.
— "*The Outrigger in New Zealand and Tahiti*", J. P. S. Vol. XXXVI, pp. 363—365.
Smith, G. Elliot: *The Influence of Ancient Egyptian Culture in the East and in America*, Reprint from the Bulletin of the John Rylands Library, Jan.-Mar., 1916.
Smith, S. Percy: *Hawaiki*, Wellington, 1903.
Stack, J.: *South Island Maoris*, Wellington, 1898.
Stair, J. B.: *Old Samoa*, 1897.
Steinen, K. von den: *Die Marquesaner und ihre Kunst*, Berlin, 1925.
Stewart, C. S.: *A Visit to the South Seas in the U. S. Ship "Vincennes" During the Years 1829 and 1831*, New York, 1832. (H. M).
— *Journal of a Residence in the Sandwich Islands During 1823, 4 and 5*, 1826.
Stolpe, H.: *Über die Tätowierung der Oster-Insulaner*, (im Königl. Zool. u. Anthropologisch-Ethnographischen Museum zu Dresden), Vol. 8, Berlin, 1899.
Sullivan, L.: "The Racial Diversity of the Polynesian Poeples", A. A. A. S., 1921, Vol. XVI, p. 518.

Tasman, A. J.: *Voyages of Abel Tasman in 1642.* (in Dalyrymple, A.: *An Historical Collection of the Several Voyages and Discoveries in the South Pacific Ocean,* London, 1770—1771.)

Thompson, B.: *The Fijians,* London, 1908.

Tregear, E.: *The Maori Race,* Wanganui, N. Z., 1904.

— "Maori and Hawaiian Kindred". J. P. S., Vol. IV, p. 203.

Turnball, J.: *Voyage around the World,* London, 1807. (H).

Turner, G.: *Samoa,* London, 1884.

Tyerman, D., and Bennett, G.: *Journal of Voyages and Travels,* 1832. (H), (T).

Vancouver, G.: *A Voyage of Discovery to the N. Pacific Ocean and round the World* .... *in 1790, 1, 2, 3, 4, and 5, in the "Chatham" and "Discovery",* in 3 vol., London, 1798.

Vason, G.: *An Authentic Narrative of Four Years Residence at Tonga-Tabu,* 1810.

Walpole, F.: *Four Years in the Pacific,* 1849. (T, S, H).

West, T.: *Ten Years in S. C. Polynesia,* 1865. (Tonga).

White, J.: *The Ancient History of the Maori,* London, 1889.

Wilkes, C. S.: *"Narrative of the U. S. Exploring Expedition during the years 1838, 9, 40, 1 and 2,"* London 1852. (S. T).

Williams, H. W.: "The Maori Whare", J. P. S., Vol. V., 1896, p. 145—154.

Williams, T., and Calvert, J.: *Fiji and the Fijians:* Edited by G. S. Row, New York, 1859.

Williamson, R. W.: *The Social and Political Systems of Central Polynesia,* Cambridge, 1924.

Wilson, J.: *A Missionary Voyage to the S. P. Ocean,* London, 1799.

Young, L.: *The Real Hawaii: Its History and Present Condition, including the True Story of the Revolution,* New York, 1899.

AVAILABLE BIBLIOGRAPHIES.

Central Polynesia	Vol. I. Williamson, R. W.
Hawaii	Brigham, W. T.: "A List of Books published at or Relating to the Hawaiian Islands" Haw. Club Paper, Oct. 1868, p. 63.
	Illingworth, J. F.: *Early References to Haw. Entomology,* B. P. Bishop Museum Bul. 2.
Maori	Collier, J.: *The Literature Relating to New Zealand.*
	Hamilton, A.: *Hand List of Certain Papers Relating more or less Directly to the Maori Race and Published in Various Publications",* T. N. Z. I., Vol. 33, 1900, pp. 515—537.
	Hocken, T. M.: *A Bibliography of the Literature Relating to New Zealand,* 1909. Government Printer.
Marquesas	Handy, E. S. C.: *The Native Culture of the Marquesas,* B. P. Bishop Museum Bul. No. 7, 1923.
Morioris	Skinner, H. D.: *The Morioris of Chatham Island,* Mem. B. P. Bishop Museum, Vol. IX, No. 1.
Samoa	Krämer, A.: *Die Samoa-Inseln,* Vol. II, Stuttgart, 1902.
Easter	Routledge, Mrs. Scoresby: *The Mystery of Easter Island,* London, 1919.